THE TAROT BOOK

THE
TAROT
BOOK

Basic Instruction
for Reading Cards

by
JANA RILEY

SAMUEL WEISER, INC.

York Beach, Maine

First published in 1992 by
Samuel Weiser, Inc.
PO Box 612
York Beach, Maine 03910

01 00

10 9 8 7 6 5

Library of Congress Cataloging-in-Publication Data
Riley, Jana, 1947–
    The Tarot book : basic instruction for reading cards / Jana
Riley
        p.   cm.
    Includes bibliographical references.
    1. Tarot.   I. Title.
    BF1879.T2R55 1992
    133.3'2424--dc20   91–29396
                                                                    CIP

ISBN 0-87728-723-6
CCP

Cover illustration: "The Magician,"
from the Crowley Thoth Tarot deck

Typeset in 11 pt. Goudy Old Style

Printed in the United States of America

The paper used in this publication meets the minimum requirements of the American National Standard for Permanence of
Paper for Printed Library Materials Z39.48-1984.

To my son, Ryan Bardach, and
to my parents, Raymond and Dean Riley,
who helped teach me about the tarot
by being Love.

Contents

Author's Note

In many ways this is not a typical tarot textbook. The subject is covered from an archetypal holistic viewpoint, bringing together the philosophies of psychology, the Qaballah, astrology, cartomancy, and an expanded archetypal theory into one single system. Carl Jung said that archetypes reside in the collective unconscious where all personal unconscious has access to the same universal material. Each of us may interpret this material according to our own perceptions, using symbols that most resonate with our own reality, but the essence of Divine Unity remains the same.

In 1888, a group of people in England began a secret society known as the Hermetic Order of the Golden Dawn. The society itself lasted only a short time, but it provides the foundation for most modern tarot decks and interpretations. In one way or another, what is now known as the Golden Dawn System is incorporated into many tarot decks of the 20th century. It is because of its synergetic scope that the Golden Dawn System has endured. It shows to us that most divinatory systems are really just different ways of saying the same thing.

My wish is that readers get as much enjoyment out of reading this book as I did out of writing it. May it bring to the spirit an Ace of Wands, to the heart a 9 of Cups, to the mind a 6 of Swords, and to the body an 8 of Discs.

CHAPTER 1

The Archetypes

The tarot is a deck of cards consisting of 78 pictures of archetypes. It is broken down into three sections:

The Major Arcana—22 cards showing archetypal forces, usually depicted as people drawn from mythology or religious traditions.

The Minor Arcana—40 cards consisting of four suits each numbered 1 through 10.

The Court Cards—16 cards depicting a King, Queen, Prince, and Princess of each of the four suits.

Before any serious discussion of the tarot is undertaken, it is probably appropriate to first try to agree upon exactly what it is we are looking at. The tarot, although familiar to cartomancers and students of the esoteric, still remains largely unknown or misunderstood in the minds of the general public. It is not uncommon to hear it called pure rubbish, wishful thinking, fortunetelling, even a tool of the devil.

But no matter how people feel about the tarot, whether they see it as a respectable form of divination or as silly superstition, it remains clear that cards—whether they be tarot or the tarot's sibling, playing cards—have some sort of formidable allurement for the mind; not only have cards been around for centuries, but they continue to be one of humanity's favorite pastimes.

Our interest in cards throughout history seems to be based on more than just our natural love of games. If it were only for this reason that cards have endured, then we would not still have the tarot, which has remained so consistently true to its original art forms. Tarot is very much like some other games we still play today, such as chess, backgammon, and checkers—they continue to carry the ancient symbols from which they originally sprang. If we explore the reason for tarot's timeless form, we discover it is not a fluke that cards have remained popular in the collective psyche of humanity, but instead—because the tarot (and playing cards) carry ageless images—they are expressions, literal pictures, of what Carl Jung called the eternal archetype.

The tarot is a collection of 78 archetypes; playing cards use 52. In reality, we can probably assume that there are an infinite number of archetypes existing in the universe, or if you take a more holistic approach, you might say the universe is one big archetype of which we perceive infinite parts; we call these perceived parts of the One different archetypes.

What is truly amazing about the tarot *is* its holism. At some point in our history, someone, or group of someones, had enough wisdom and knowledge of dimensions beyond our own to set down in picture cards 78 of these universal archetypes. How someone managed to do so with such faithful, unerring precision is an enigma that remains to this day one of history's unanswerable puzzles.

So what is an archetype? Carl Gustav Jung, one of the greatest psychologists of our time, is the person responsible for defining in modern terminology what an archetype is. Even though examples of archetypes have been with us from the beginning in such familiar traditions as games, religion, mythology, legends, folklore, and fairy tales, as well as the esoteric arts (such as astrology, numerology, geomancy, and cartomancy), Carl Jung is responsible for bringing to us descriptions and knowledge of archetypes which are acceptable to our current way of thinking. His theories and ideas have done much to change the foundation of psychology as we know it today. Jung spoke of truths that touched our hearts and sparked within us the recognition of something we thought we had lost.

An archetype is a difficult concept to define with any of the five senses. Sight, hearing, and even communication through the spoken or written word all become inadequate when attempting to define archetypes. Because archetypes are holistic, able to encompass worlds both visible and invisible, both physical and spiritual, by their very nature, they are ephemeral, like footprints left in the sand or wisps of shadows glimpsed for a moment just beyond our periphery of vision. They are not bound by time or space, past or future, and they play in dimensions most of us can only dream of.

We may recognize an archetype by the tracks it makes, by the effect it leaves in our lives in the form of strange incidents, revelations, or magical moments. Jung defined such a moment of archetypal recognition as a synchronicity. A more popular definition of recognizing an archetype might be a startling coincidence.

Carl Jung dedicated his life to this search for the "something not perceived." He wrote of archetypes:

> The collective unconscious is a part of the psyche which can be negatively distinguished from a personal unconscious by the fact that it does not, like the latter, owe its existence to personal experience and consequently it is not a personal acquisition. While the personal unconscious is made up essentially of contents which have at one time been conscious but which have disappeared from consciousness through having been forgotten or repressed, the contents of the collective unconscious have never been in consciousness, and therefore have never been individually acquired, but owe their existence exclusively to heredity. Whereas the personal unconsciousness consists for the most part of *complexes*, the content of the collective unconscious is made up essentially of *archetypes*.

The concept of the archetype . . . indicates the existence
of definite forms in the psyche which seem to be present
always and everywhere.

[The instincts] . . . form very close analogies to the
archetypes, so close, in fact, that there is good reason for
supposing that the archetypes are the unconscious
images of the instincts themselves, in other words, that
they are *patterns of instinctual behaviour*.[1]

Jung probably remains unsurpassed in his research and
exploration of archetypes as applied to the human psyche.
Although he consistently made subtle referrals to the existence
of archetypes in other areas of life, the mass of his published
material deals only with the psychological aspects.

Another more mystical and less psychological way of view-
ing the archetypes is to see them as emanations originating from
the Godhead. The Godhead is one, undivided, the All-That-Is
in a state of beingness where there is *not*, for all *is*. When the
Godhead is pictured as light, as It is often described, the light is
seen to be pouring forth its rays, infiltrating all of creation with
itself. The closer the rays of light are to the source of the Godhead, the purer and less divided they are. As they descend
further from the source, the less pure and more coarse they
become, and the less they partake of is-ness. If this can be
pictured in linear time and space (which light isn't, but we must
deal with what we can understand) we can see the Godhead not
only sending forth pure rays of individual beams of Itself
through the matrices of infinitude, but also modifying these
beams at each progressive level of space according to the angles,
or arcs, at which they are perceived.

Just as water seeks its own level, the individual rays of light
beams being sent forth from the source consist of harmonically-
resonant spectrums encompassing the unique code-pattern that

[1]C.G. Jung, *The Archetypes and the Collective Unconscious*, Bollingen Series XXX, translated by R.F.C. Hull (Princeton, NJ: Princeton University Press, 1959), pp. 42–44.

the All-That-Is has programmed in each. Each spectrum is a part of the source, reflecting that part of the source which it has sent forth from itself. At each level these light-blueprints fuse or translate according to the rhythms of the plane and process they are intermeshing with, and even though they remain whole, they appear translated according to each level's perception of them. In other words, the Godhead sends images of Itself out to "become" according to each image's own innate nature.

As the groupings, or arrangements, of like light-beams reach closer to the coarser portion of the cosmos, the light eventually materializes, grounding itself in its rhythmically similar material form. Each material form is but a physical manifestation of the light-archetype from which it formed, partaking of the same code-pattern that formed it. Viewed this way, each archetype is an arrangement of energy-motion corresponding to its own like code-principle, not only on this level but on all the similar levels that oscillate with its own particular light-blueprint. This implies that constant creation is forever and in all ways taking place, all archetypes mirroring the original source, the All-That-Is as it spirals down from the purest of matrices. Each archetype is the same energy-motion comprised of the origin, structure, and dynamics of its own light ray from the source. This also implies that the source is creating life from itself, and life is also creating the source from itself.

Although Jung limited his analysis to the human mind and spirit, couching his interpretations in psychological-sociological terms more easily acceptable to the scientific communities, this universal principle is an alternate description of archetypes as applied to the human psyche. He simply said it differently, more psychically.

Webster's Ninth New Collegiate Dictionary defines an archetype as "the original pattern or model of which all things of the same type are representations or copies." If we consider Jung's psychological theory that archetypes comprise the collective unconscious, the mystical theory of archetypes being light-beams of God encoded with God Itself, and take into account

Webster's definition that archetypes are copies of the original model, we may find ourselves recalling the ancient philosophy known as Taoism. Taoists say that all is one, and any idea we have that anything is unique or set apart from anything else is merely illusion, stemming from our ability to perceive only a small part of any whole.

Included within this concept is the symbolism of the microcosm and macrocosm, the macrocosm being God, the microcosms being what we are calling archetypes. Everything is contained within everything else, i.e., the quark is within the electron, the electron within the atom, the atom within the molecule, the molecule within the cell, the cell within the organ, the organ within the body, the body within the earth, earth within the solar system, the solar system within the galaxy, the galaxy within the universe, and on and on ad infinitum, both inward as well as outward. Just because an atom is not aware of the organ it is in, as we are not aware of the molecules within us, does not mean that they are separate or do not exist. It means that we cannot know of one another because of our lack of awareness.

If we view the infinite number of microcosms in a single macrocosm as archetypes, we might better say that we are not aware of them because we are only able to perceive at angles compatible to our own. It is no accident that Plato knew about archetypes two millennia ago, and even called them such, because *archetypes are the type of angle, or arch, in which we view the Whole*. When we read cards, whether we know it or not, we are studying various angles of other various angles, according to their own angle. Of course, this is true of everyone and everything, but what makes divination unique is that we are attempting to grasp angles which extend beyond our present ones; we are admitting, hopefully, that the world extends beyond that of which we are aware.

There are numerous ways of describing the archetypes, and through the ages people have done so in every way imaginable. But if we can read between the lines, we will discover all these seemingly different descriptions are more or less saying the same thing. Tarot cards do it with pictures. And seldom has the expression "a picture is worth a thousand words" been more applicable than in tarot.

• • •

Most tarot decks use people to depict the archetypes. Over the ages so much effort and research have gone into the human figures of the Major Arcana, not to mention their surrounding symbols, that the Major of many decks speaks volumes of information through its currently understood symbolism. However, this does not appear to be the case with the Minor Arcana and court cards.

It is natural enough that the court cards should be people in tarot. The only symbolism we need from them is that of showing exactly what kind of people we are talking about. But the Minor Arcana is an altogether different story because the Minor is not only talking about people; it is instead more like the Major than the court cards in that it attempts to show an infinitude of universal possibilities and archetypes. The Minor Arcana of most decks uses people to depict the wholeness of life, but there are some decks which also employ more cosmogonal symbolism.

For instance, playing cards use numbers, color, and arrangement of pips to depict universal meaning. And the Crowley (Thoth) deck is a fascinating representation of archetypes expressed not only by number but also as unifying coagencies and code-patterns. Lady Freida Harris, who painted the deck under Aleister Crowley's direction, used mandalas, symmetries, and color to express the archetypes in the Minor Arcana. For example, Crowley's 2 of Discs shows a crowned serpent looping around itself into a figure 8 with two yin-yang symbols within each loop of the 8. One could hardly conceive of a more harmonious representation in a single picture for the 2 of Discs, expressing both its exoteric meaning (juggling the dualities of everyday living) combined with its esoteric meaning (opposites being the two halves of the same circle, implying no polarity within polarity). The symbolism and imagery in the Crowley deck is an exciting and enlightening pansophy of the archetypes expressed in brilliant symbolism.

This difference between expressing archetypes as people or expressing them as symbols is significant. In tarot, because we are attempting to interpret the wholeness of life from a few pictures painted onto cards, it is important that we not limit ourselves any more than we already, by necessity, are. Archetypes are not only people—they are all of life everywhere—people, animals, nature, emotions, thoughts, spirit, events, and situations. To limit pictures or words to only people is like trying to describe the ocean by looking at one drop of water. In this sense, tarot decks depicting the archetypes as symmetries, manadalas, and universal symbols are usually more accurate than those using only people.

This is especially true of the Minor Arcana because, as mentioned, while the Major Arcana over the centuries has lent itself to archetypal analyses and symbology expressing wholeness, the Minor Arcana is still sadly lacking in many decks. Not only is the totality of the archetype lost in its picture of human dominance, but all too often the card's picture leads the student to view only one side of its human condition, with its polarity being completely ignored.

This is not to imply that people symbology in the Minor Arcana is always more limited than those using symmetrical arrangements or code symbols, but it can be the case. As a matter of fact, there are some decks available now with Minor Arcana that are outstanding in the way they have incorporated symbology on and around people. If we focus only on people, however, we may tend to forget we are not alone in the universe, that God is all creatures and all life, and in tarot there is nothing that can be said, told, or predicted for ourselves or others that does not in some major way involve all that is around us.

In religion, archetypes are often called devils, gods, angels, and demons. In mythology they are heroes, heroines, and objects of power. Archetypes are in all things, and express in all ways—people and objects included. But it is as incorrect to think of them as *only* entities (i.e., people or animals) as it is to think of them as *only* spirits or demons. For while they are these entities, they are also the processes and motion of *all* things. Archetypes are arrangements of processes and motion; they are dynamic oscillating motion grouped and ordered by like-rhythms. Just as in physics the sub-atomic world consists not only of particles but also of waves, so in the physical world and beyond, archetypes consist not only of entities but also of processes.

Archetypes are processes, or symmetries, of harmonically-resonant energy-motion. They are matrices of concordant form and motion, never static, corresponding to and intermeshing with lattices of like motion. When we spot a synchronicity, we are recognizing an archetype breaking in from another spectrum, or dimension, to complete itself in time-space.

Although he doesn't use the word archetype, in his book *Notes to my Children*, Ken Carey gives a delightful description of archetypes as found within people. To briefly summarize, he says that if we watch a river flowing, we will notice many little ripples and whirlpools in the river. When the flowing river passes rapidly over something under the water, strange patterns are formed. But what are they really, these patterns? Apart from the water, there is no definite entity in the pattern, for every instant the pattern consists of different and new drops of water. In some places where there is a rock buried beneath the surface of the water, a pattern is formed that lasts, so that it remains a fixed pattern. It appears to be a thing of itself. In reality, however, it is a part of the river, constantly renewed by the river's flow, so that eventually the entire river may flow through this pattern. Whirlpools are created, which for a time form a powerful force of their own, until they eventually get swept back into the river's flow.[2]

---

[2]Ken Carey, *Notes to My Children: A Simplified Metaphysics* (Kansas City, MO: Uni-Sun, 1984), pp. 81–82.

This is a difficult concept to grasp, to think of ourselves as whirlpools within a river. But whether we realize it or not, like water within water, we humans are more of a process than an entity, and we cannot separate ourselves from the processes, or archetypes, anymore than the whirlpool can separate itself from the river. In rivers, air, people, and in all things, there is no fundamental reduction base because all things are wholes within the part and parts within the whole.

We attempt to perceive with our two-dimensional awareness what is in actuality spanning innumerable realities. It is like asking an insect to know why it is sprayed with poison or smashed with a foot when it is just sitting there on an ordinary day minding its own business as it has always done. Perhaps it did perceive our presence as a shadow cast like a dark cloud upon the surface of the wall where it sat just before its death, much like the way a person may scarcely perceive a thought cast across the mind just prior to its physical occurrence.

Jung said that the archetypes are both unknown and all-knowing; they are inside us, outside us, in us, and we are in them. They are all consciousness, and their symmetries overlap and interpenetrate one another in such multifaceted complexity that their magnitudes extend into the point as well as into the circumference of all. They cannot be separated from one another entirely, as they are the part of the whole, and the whole of the part, as all things.

When we read the tarot, we are attempting to become aware, as humbly and incompletely as it may be, of the intrinsic qualities and action of the archetypes. We are taking 78 images upon cards, and saying, "I know you are what I cannot know, but I cannot not know you." We can say of the tarot images as Ernest Hemmingway's hero said at the end of the movie, *Islands in the Stream*, "I now know that no one thing is true—it is all true."

CHAPTER 2

The Tarot and Synchronicity

Essentially, the tarot is the same as a deck of regular playing cards with only two exceptions—the tarot deck includes the Major Arcana and playing cards don't; the tarot has four court cards per suit while playing cards have only three.

It is an ongoing debate among researchers as to which came first, the tarot or playing cards. Because the origin of the tarot is shrouded in uncertainty and mysticism, it is likely that much of its history will continue to remain a mystery to us. Historians like to point out that playing cards have been around long before any evidence of the tarot came upon the scene, but historians rely largely on the written word and physical evidence to form their conclusions, and since the tarot, by its very nature, was likely to have remained hidden in temples and in the hands of the knowledgeable who wished to keep it secret, it is possible that it was unobtainable or unknown to the general public for some time, thus making tangible physical evidence difficult to produce.

Whatever their history may be, both the tarot and playing cards still speak pretty much the same language. We know that since at least the 14th century both decks have been used for gaming, and in some parts of the world the tarot is still used and played as a card game. And both decks have been and are still used as a source of divination.

Other than the Major Arcana and the court cards, the basic difference between the two decks is that the tarot receives bad press while playing cards are considered okay. The obvious reason for this is because the tarot is associated with divination, while playing cards are associated with games and gambling. Whereas games and gambling are a favorite pastime in our society, divination has taken the opposite track, suffering almost fanatic disapproval at the hands of church and state. Divination has long been a source of discontent to whoever or whatever is currently in authority, for it takes the source of power away from the establishment and places it into the hands of the individual. One may reasonably argue that it is good that churches, government, and socially approved institutions stand as guardians of judgment because, as they are quick to point out, the individual can be no judge of himself, but on the other hand, we can just as reasonably argue that neither can anyone else be the judge of the individual.

•   •   •

Although the tarot and playing card decks may have evolved differently, it is assumed that they evolved along the same lines, more or less. This is readily apparent by their obvious similarities. Both decks share many of the same common numerical synchronicities—both have four suits, ten pip cards, and court cards. In other ways their similarities are clearly more separate from one another, each deck's characteristics corresponding to its own somewhat different and unique evolution. They contain within their symbolism both esoteric and exoteric synchronicities—or coincidences—that relate to human beings as we have unfolded and interpreted our place in the universe.

In chapter 1 we discussed that the cards are pictures of the archetypes, and that an archetype is a symmetry of energy-motion. Put another way, we may say that *an archetype is motion plus form* because its symmetry is its form and its energy is its motion. On the cards, it is the *form* of the archetype that the artist is attempting to depict to the best of his ability, and in divination it is the *motion* of the archetypes we are attempting to read. But it is not only in cards that archetypes display their motion and form, for if we look closely, we can see the evidence of archetypes around us all the time in literally everything that exists.

Actually, everything is motion and form, but we perceive only the tiniest fraction of either, if we perceive them at all. I use the word *form* to indicate all things material, physical, symmetrical, or moving as a group—as anything kept glued together by its attraction to self has some sort of form, whether that be an atom, an elephant, or a thought. It may be said that there really are no such things as separate forms *per se*, that all is motion, form merely being the order of the motion, or a particular angle in which we are perceiving energy.

An archetype is, literally speaking, not separated from others or itself by form but is perceived as such by the angle in which we are seeing a certain portion of the whole, usually that angle we perceive as most like ourselves. This is why the word *archetype* has the same meaning and root derivative as the words *archangel, angel, angle, arc, arch, arcane, arkana, arkanum,* and *aura*. Angels are but angles, and archetypes are but arcs. The whole is largely hidden from us because of our angle, which is why when something is hidden or secretive it is said to be arcane. When we study the tarot, or the Major and Minor Arcanas, in effect, we are studying the different angels, or angles, which affect and determine our destinies.

Jung coined the term *synchronicity* to define those times when we occasionally recognize a fragment of archetypal presence. He said that certain things like to happen together in time:

Synchronicity [is] . . . the meaningful coincidence or equivalence (*a*) of a psychic and a physical state or event which [appear to] have no causal relationship to one another. . . . (b) of similar or identical thoughts, dreams, etc. occurring at the same time in different places.[1]

Psychologically speaking, synchronicity can be defined as certain similar things or events happening together in time that do not appear to be causally related. Those of us not familiar with the word *synchronicity* are most certainly familiar with the word *coincidence*. We all go through life saying and hearing the exclamation, "What a coincidence!" In reality, synchronicity and coincidence are synonomous, although when we use the word *coincidence* we tend to think of it being a result of pure chance, whereas with synchronicity we are implying some sort of purpose and intent, and the only chance involved is a fat one.

Even though synchronicities in the psychological sense are often thought of as being inclusive of a defined time-period, this is not always the case. Synchronicity is in actuality the indication of the presence of an archetype in motion, and since archetypes work through and in all levels, including those in which there is no time nor space, we can define synchronicity as being whenever any archetypal pattern is consciously observed, regardless of time or space, resulting in what we call a coincidence. For instance, a woman may marry a man named Bill, divorce him, and twenty years later marry another man named Bill. Or a man may be involved in an automobile accident in Los Angeles, and the same week his sister may also be in an accident in New York City.

In the scientific sense, examples of sychronicities are generally held to be unique and rare, and such appears to be the case in the more spectacular and miraculous ones. Indeed, what we call a miracle is nothing other than an example of a spectacular synchronicity. But once we become aware of archetypal presences, we see that synchroncities are not at all rare; in fact, the world abounds in coincidence. They are with us in our most common everyday living and experiences. After becoming

---

[1]C.G. Jung, *Memories, Dreams, Reflections* (New York: Random House, 1961), p. 400.

aware that an archetype is a harmonically-resonant symmetry at all levels, certain events are seen to occur not because they are coincidences, but because they are the very foundation of our entire universe, and it becomes impossible not to see shadows of larger unknown archetypes stepping into our realities everywhere we turn. The more we watch them, the more they are recognized, until it becomes a matter of not knowing where they begin or end. Which, of course, they don't.

Life processes occur in similar rhythms that are resonant to their own individual natures. In other words, like attracts like, thus forming symmetries of like-motion. This is such an obvious statement that it is for the most part ignored. All things that we know have to originate and act from their own personal resonance because of the law, like attracts like. They cannot do otherwise. It does not even occur to us that they could do otherwise, and if they ever did, it would truly be a miracle of such unbelievable proportions that life as we know it would be turned upside down. A tree sends its roots to be nourished by the earth and its leaves to be fed by the sun, and we would never expect to see the opposite—a tree with its roots in the air and its leaves in the earth. Nature shows us common archetypes.

But there are also those symmetries of like-motion where we are not able to identify exactly what likeness is drawing to itself because we can't see the whole archetype. We are only aware of the effect without its associated cause. A common synchronicity occurs when one light bulb blows out—shortly thereafter a few more light bulbs also go out. After a while you learn to buy more than one light bulb when you go to the store. Or have you sat at home with not a thing to do? For hours (or days) you can be bored, bored, bored. If you call your friends, none of them are at home, or they're busy. But when you finally get occupied with something that truly entertains you, that you don't want to quit for anything, the phone will start ringing, and friends come out of the woodwork. Or your children will come home sick from school on the same day your mate comes home early from work and wants both dinner and attention *now*, U.P.S. will deliver a package, and a neighbor will stop by to chat. We even have sayings to express synchronicities like these, such as "When it rains, it pours," or, "It's either feast or famine."

When planning your vacation it doesn't make one wit of difference how carefully you have done all your work and painstakingly managed to get "all caught up" in order to leave your desk clean; mere hours before your scheduled departure all heck will break loose, and you will find yourself suddenly facing a work crisis only you are able to solve. These moments of synchronicity have been amusingly labeled "Murphy's Law."

How many times have you met a person with a certain name—perhaps a name you haven't personally heard in years—only to hear or read that name over and over again in the next few days or weeks? Or the type of car, kind of dog, or anything that repeats itself after you have encountered it once? Suddenly, it is everywhere you turn, even though you know it wasn't there before.

And then there is the familiar conversation with an acquaintance when he says, "That's funny, I was just talking (or thinking) about that same thing." We have all thought of someone just before the phone rings, and that same someone is calling. Or we have dreamed of a certain person or recalled that person only to have him or her appear in our lives a short time later.

Synchronicities, or coincidences where you can only recognize the effect of the archetype and not the cause, are everywhere—in birth and death dates of friends and family, hitting every red light or green light while driving (usually depending on whether or not you are in a hurry), the names of people you know and have known (names of people we know personally are usually the same, similar, or rhyme with one another, and often have the same root meaning), and in a "streak of good luck" or a "run of bad luck." The list is endless, for archetypal behavior expressed in synchronicities is infinite.

To say that certain things like to happen together in time or that a pattern is seen to repeat itself regardless of time and space are other ways of saying that an archetype is being recognized through its effect. We cannot but perceive its shadow, its breath, as it passes through our reality. What the bigger picture may mean is lost to us as we glimpse only the tiniest sameness of its wholeness in a coincidence.

Yet, when we observe similar common correspondences in our lives, like the way the car magically starts when we turn the key, or like the way every baby always manages to take its first step, or certain patterns in our lives that seem to repeat themselves over and over again, we don't consider these coincidences. These, and countless others, are such commonly known rhythms that are corresponding and functioning through their own like-vibrations that we don't even think about synchronicities being involved in their functions. Not for a moment do we consider it a coincidence that rain falls from a cloud or that light comes from the sun. We just take it for granted that that is how things work. We say we understand them, but this is only because we believe that we comprehend their associations with each other—their "like-patterns" of similarity. The only difference between these commonly accepted like-patterns that are everywhere all around us in everything, and the coincidence, or synchronicity, is that in the coincidence we aren't aware of the whole picture. We aren't aware of all the associations taking place, and so it appears as a puzzle to us—an unknown, a mystery.

It is when we *don't* understand something and how it works that we call it a coincidence or a synchronicity. Just because we aren't perceiving the full picture doesn't mean there isn't one. A coincidence means that, unlike clouds and rain, we don't know all that is being enacted or involved in its full unfoldment. When we don't understand certain agreeing-archetypes in their full arrangement, we call the fragments of behavior that we do recognize synchronicities. An archetypal pattern is only termed a synchronicity when we recognize part of an unknown process at work, being unable to perceive or to comprehend the larger picture.

In the case of cards it is a synchronicity that a deck of fifty-two playing cards corresponds both numerically and by suit to the earth's relationship with the solar system, and in tarot that the Major Arcana corresponds to other divinatory systems. It is possible that someone long ago contrived all this, but more likely it is a synchronicity—human beings consciously or unconsciously responding to code-patterns that are established between ourselves and the cards.

PLAYING CARDS

Playing cards are divided into two colors—red and black. The Earth has two great divisions of the year—when the sun is north of the equator and when the sun is south of the equator.

The North Pole is Earth's electromagnetic positive pole, shown by the two black suits of spades and clubs, which are considered masculine and aggressive. The South Pole is Earth's electromagnetic negative pole, shown by the two red suits of hearts and diamonds, which are considered feminine and receptive.

There are four suits and four seasons. The two black suits, spades and clubs, symbolize fall and spring, the two masculine seasons that bring change. The two red suits, hearts and diamonds, are summer and winter, the two feminine seasons that provide stability.

Three court cards per suit with four suits equals a total of twelve court cards, the number of months in a year, and the time it takes the Earth to make one full solar cycle. There are thirteen cards per suit, and thirteen weeks per season. There are thirteen cards per suit, and the Moon has thirteen complete lunar cycles per year. There are fifty-two cards in a deck. There are fifty-two weeks in a year. Each suit has a total of ninety-one pips, the number of days in each season. If we divide ninety-one by seven (the number of days in a week) we again get thirteen, the number of cards in each suit.

If we consider the point value of each card, making the Ace count as 1, and Jacks, Queens, and Kings as 11, 12, and 13 respectively, and add up all the pips on the cards, we get 364 pips. Adding the Joker, we arrive at a total of 365, which equals the number of days in a year.

TAROT

Antonio Dragoni suggested in 1814 that the twenty-one Major Arcana (omitting the Fool) represented the perfect number 3 and the mystical number 7. Setting aside the Fool, there remain in the tarot pack seventy-seven cards, or 11 times 7. These seventy-seven cards are further divided into two classes, twenty-one emblematic cards (3 × 7) and the fifty-six Minor Arcana cards (8 × 7).[2]

There are twenty-two Major Arcana, and in astrology there are twelve zodical signs with ten rulers, for a total of twenty-two.

There are twenty-two Major Arcana and the holy Semitic (Hebrew) alphabet has twenty-two letters. The Hebrew alphabet is a complete numerical system, its letters being both letters and numbers, and is a self-encompassing divinatory system within itself. It is also believed by some to be connected with the symbols on runestones. There are ten cards per suit. On the Qabalistic Tree of Life (the mystical branch of Judaism) there are ten spheres called Sephiroth. There are twenty-two Major Arcana. On the Qabalistic Tree of Life there are twenty-two connecting Paths of Wisdom.

•   •   •

It's interesting to note that playing cards have numerical correspondences correlating to more commonly understood pat-

---

[2]Stuart R. Kaplan, *The Encyclopedia of Tarot*, vol. 1 (Stamford, CT: U.S. Games Systems, 1983), p. 14.

terns, while the tarot seems to possess numerical correspondences more significant to scholars of deeper esoteric study,
which is in perfect accord with the cards themselves. Playing
cards are used largely for gaming and more ordinary purposes,
and draw to themselves the simpler, more common, synchronicities. On the other hand, tarot cards attract numerical correspondences more in line with their energies of more complex,
but lesser known, symmetries.

When relating to synchronistic numbers in the cards, we are
working with but a few of the indeterminable multitude of patterns that archetypes display. Numbers display vast synchronicities and were believed to be the key to the formula of the
universe by such founding fathers of mathematics as Plato,
Pythagoras, Tycho, Galileo, and Kepler. Certain sequences of
the primary numbers go back into themselves over and over
again, always interchanging with the same sequences, supposedly into infinity. As with all things, they create themselves out
of themselves. Even though only a few numerical synchronicities found in the cards are mentioned here, it should be appreci-
ated that numbers in general outdo themselves in their overall
affinity to displaying archetypal synchronicities.

•   •   •

Because of the unlimited ability of all archetypes to re-
create, re-structure and re-integrate themselves, it is impossible
to say just how many archetypes actually exist. It is certainly
beyond human scope to comprehend such vastness. When it
comes to knowing just exactly how many archetypes there may
be and how it is that they interact and form within one another,
not only is it impossible for us to separate the wheat from the
chaff, but it is also impossible to know just how much wheat or
chaff there may be.

In the particular instance of tarot and playing cards, we
have limited our interpretation of archetypes to either fifty-two
(playing cards) or seventy-eight (tarot). Although the number of

cards for both decks has varied throughout the centuries and throughout different cultures, fifty-two and seventy-eight has pretty much remained the accepted number in the Western world for the last five or six hundred years.

There is, however, the very strong possibility that two more archetypal blueprints are now in the process of evolving in the tarot. There is much supposition to suggest the existence of at least two more Major Arcana heretofore unknown, and some research has even been done. Not only in the tarot and other mystical sciences, but also in the rhythm of the Earth's daily cycle, strong evidence exists to support the theory that where there are only twenty-two identified archetypes, there were once twenty-four, or that there will be twenty-four. Certainly, as far as archetypes are concerned, twenty-four is no more of a magical *total* than any other number, as the overall total cannot ever be known for sure, but it may be that as far as our awareness of archetypes is concerned, twenty-two is now ready to evolve to the next logical step of twenty-four. Twenty-four is part of the Earth's cycle, as evidenced by the 24-hour clock.

We find the first indication that twenty-four is an important number in the esoteric sciences themselves. For instance, in modern astrology there are two missing planets. Currently, astrology has twelve signs that describe twelve sets of twin characteristics. Each of these twelve signs possesses the positive and negative of its own innate nature, making the twelve signs into a total of twenty-four manifestations. Astrology also uses twelve houses for each of the twelve signs. The astrologer, for the purposes of a geocentric natal chart, assumes that Earth is a fixed point and all other cosmic bodies revolve around it once a day. He or she then applies this 24-hour system to the birth chart. The chart is divided into twelve segments, or houses, and one segment, or house, equals 2 hours out of the total of 24 hours. The big problem with all this is that at this time there are only nine known planets (and the sun and moon) to rule these twelve signs and twelve houses. This gives us a total of twenty-two, but leaves us with the suspicion that there ought to be twenty-four.

Many astrologers think there are two missing planets. In order to deal with this contrary dilemma, they have given the two missing planets the same names as two already known-existing planets, making Mercury the ruler of both Virgo and Gemini, and Venus the ruler of both Taurus and Libra. There has been a great deal of debate over this, but until the other two planets are discovered, astrologers have simply (or not so simply) given the same planet to two different signs, attributing completely different characteristics to the same planet, as the case requires. This may seem rather foolish, but actually, under the circumstances it doesn't work out all that badly, because the correct traits have at least been attributed to the correct sign, even if not to their correct planet.

We find even more evidence of two missing archetypes in the Qabalah. In tarot, the Qaballistic Tree of Life is drawn with twenty-two Paths of Wisdom which lead to ten Sephiroth. Collectively, the Sephiroth and Paths are called the Thirty-Two Paths of Wisdom. However, there is also an eleventh Sephira called Daath which is often not represented on the Tree because it is said to be located in the Abyss. When Daath is drawn, we again have twenty-four Paths of Wisdom because we need two paths in order to connect Daath to the tree.[3]

Not all esoteric traditions have lost the two missing archetypes. In the sacred art of casting runes, there are twenty-five stones, but one of those is blank, which, you guessed it, leaves us with a total of twenty-four. And in playing cards there are twelve court cards. Each of these cards has two portraits on it—each inverted to the other, so there are twenty-four faces on all court cards in a playing deck.

---

[3]The reader should refer to the works by Clifford Bias, William Gray, Aryeh Kaplan, and Robert Wang for further information on the Sephira of the Tree of Life. Daath is considered by Qabalists to be very much present on the tree, even though it is sometimes represented in the Abyss.

Leaving esoteric tradition for a moment and moving on to more mundane indicators in our search for twenty-four archetypes, as previously mentioned, we find another key when we consider time, and the twenty-four hour day. We measure yearly, monthly, and weekly time by the cycles of the Earth in relation to the sun, as evidenced by the calendar, and we also base daily cycles on the sun's units of twenty-four as evidenced by the clock. The Earth rotates every 23 hours 56 minutes (the siderial day) and this is the basis of clock time.

We work with this twenty-four hour day, and break it into twelve hours of light from the sun and twelve hours of dark (as measured from the Earth's center—the equator).

Earth has a 23-1/2° tilt. The apparent yearly path of the sun in the sky is known as the ecliptic. The ecliptic is the projection of the plane of Earth's orbit onto the celestial sphere. Because of Earth's 23-1/2° tilt, the angle between the ecliptic and the celestial equator is also 23-1/2°. The two intersect at the vernal equinox (0 Aries) and the autumnal equinox (0 Libra).

In the tarot, there are some possibilities for two missing archetypes. The latest and smaller edition of Crowley's Thoth deck contains two extra cards by Lady Harris—a second version of The Magus and a third version titled "The Magician."[4] Gary Ross, the editor of *Tarot Network News*, suggests that these two cards may correspond to the Neurogenetic Tarot. Crowley's additional Magician would correspond to 000 Fusion, relating to Chiron, and the alternate Magus would correspond to 00 Starmaker, relating to Persephone.[5] A key word might be "order" for Fusion and "force" for Starmaker.

If we feel so inclined, we could begin to work with these two additional archetypal figures now by using the new Crowley

---

[4]These two Major Arcana are available in the small Crowley deck published by Urania Verlag and U.S. Games, Inc.; they can be obtained from Samuel Weiser.

[5]Gary Ross discusses "the Neurogenetic Tarot described by Timothy Leary and Robert Anton Wilson in their book *The Game of Life*," (Scotsdale, AZ: Falcon Press, 1992) in the article, "The Three-Dimensional Tree of Life," *Tarot Network News*, ed. Gary Ross, Spring 1985, pp. 16–18. Also see *TNN*, Supplement 3, Spring 1988, p. 3.

deck or by making our own Fusion and Starmaker with other
decks. It would be interesting to see if they unfold recognizable
archetypal patterns that we can get in touch with, and if so, how
they affect us.

It may be that in the Major Arcana we use today we are
missing representations of certain archetypes. Whether this is a
modern loss or an ancient one we don't know. Perhaps the
ancients did not pass their knowledge on to us, or perhaps
recognition of certain additional archetypes is just now coming
to mass consciousness. Some people believe the remaining two
factors that help us evolve to the next step of twenty-four will be
discovered when we are ready to move on to higher
development.

CHAPTER 3

The Tarot and the Individual

We have always been able to look at life through ourselves or through others: most people look at life through others. While they look to others for both good and evil, basing judgments on personal appraisal and reactions of other people, students of the esoteric look within and base their judgments on what they find inside themselves. The irony is that, when asked, we usually label ourselves the opposite of who we really are. Many people confidently believe they understand themselves, while the eso- teric types often believe they have failed at self-realization. When we project onto other people, believing that we are seeing them, we are in reality only seeing ourselves in them. It is better to look within so that we end up more clearly seeing others—not as reflections of ourselves—but as they really are.

It is human nature to look to others for both our answers and our questions, our problems and our solutions. That is why we have leaders, churches, governments, heroes, and peer groups. They tell us what we should do, what is right, what is wrong, and we set certain people up as role models upon which to pattern our own lives. We sometimes believe we are seeing clearly when we join a certain church and embrace its tenets, when we vote Republican or Democrat, and when we choose certain actors, actresses, or public figures to look up to and admire, or else to look down on and scorn, but in reality, all of this is merely ourselves projecting what we believe onto some- one else and has little to do with what that person really is.

Students of life seldom belong to any religious institution because they know its tenets always flow from its leaders' personal beliefs, and they seldom attach much importance to public figures because they know that how the politicians perceive themselves and how the public perceive them is usually false.

This is also the case with tarot. Tarot can be seen from within or from without; the choice is ours. Some see tarot as something to project outwardly into the environment rather than inwardly. After studying for a while these people believe themselves knowledgeable of both self and others, then set out to use the knowledge on others. The problem with this theory is that learning is a lifetime endeavor, actually probably many lifetimes, and whenever we take what little we have learned and start projecting it out onto others, we are once again falling into the trap of not seeing anyone clearly—them or us. Eventually we have to choose either the fortunetelling approach to tarot where we advise others, or the more individual approach where we use its symbolism for personal growth and understanding.

Some people think they have achieved enlightenment when they cease to belong to a church, or make idols out of people. Hopefully, this is a step in the right direction, but there is a real danger here, especially in the world of esoteric study, because some people merely end up just transferring their idols from other people to themselves. They don't know this is what they are doing, and often think they are following higher powers, but many times it is simply their own subconscious. We can tell the difference between benevolent higher powers and lower possibly malevolent powers because good archetypes *don't* interfere with other people's business, *don't* inflate the ego, flatter, or make us feel we are more special than anyone else, and *don't* communicate in terms of polarities, i.e., right vs. wrong, man vs. woman. Archetypes are accepting of where we are in all ways.

How is it that we can expect to define realities for other people if we have learned that they cannot define our realities for us? There is a dichotomy here, and it can be a real danger for seekers. We need to be careful that we do not merely transfer our idols from others to ourselves, so that we believe ourselves capable of giving answers to others.

If there is any one thing we should learn from divination, it is the fact that each individual walks a different path. Intellectually speaking, this is not a difficult concept to grasp. Most people feel that individual freedom is everyone's God-given right. However, to *know* something is not the same thing as to *be* something, and when it comes to actually living the belief that we are all entitled to our individual destiny, regardless of our own personal approval or disapproval of it, that is quite a different story. Thus, we have the crusaders: pro-lifers, the pro-choice, the various Christian denominations, the political activists, and such a vicissitude of causes and laws and do-gooders, each professing to be right for all, that it boggles the mind. And we have the same situation in divination—the belief that what is right for me is right for you, too. If we believe this is *any* way, if we believe that we can divine what another should or should not do in *any* way whatsoever, then we have failed to understand the single most important truth divination can teach us.

To attempt to define whether something is good or evil involves value judgments that can be seen *only* through the eyes of the individual concerned. In tarot, we may be able to recognize certain archetypes and their likely classical behaviors, but it is another story altogether to try to define just what the *purposes* of those archetypes may be. As human beings, we can always perceive only a part of any whole; although we can guess how people may express certain archetypal behavior, we cannot know the full picture of the why's and wherefore's behind that behavior. We are doing extremely well if we are in touch with our own purpose, never mind someone else's.

Let's consider a few examples. Most people agree that it isn't good to drink alcohol to the point of dysfunction. People are generally considered to be helpful and beneficial when they try to persuade others to stop drinking, to give up their ruinous addiction. If an alcoholic comes to a card reader, seeking whatever it is he or she is seeking through the cards, are we right to advise this individual to give up the addiction?

It was a reformed alcoholic who taught me that for some people, drinking is a blessing, not a curse. Her parents owned a nightclub so she grew up in the club where her parents worked. She started drinking at the age of 6 or 7. She was an abused child. Without going into all the details, she had many problems, of which drinking was only one. At age 40 she was able to give up drinking but did not get involved with therapy. She became a psychotic schizophrenic. No doubt she had always had psychotic tendencies, and the alcohol repressed the violent action that emerged when she stopped drinking.

As anybody who deals with chemically abusive people can tell you, drugs and alcohol are not the *cause* of their problems, they are the *symptoms*. It is often what we term evil, such as drugs, that is in actuality masking what is really the ultimate despair in a person, and many times the person who chooses to do drugs is doing so because, consciously or unconsciously, he or she has chosen one of the options available. If we respond by saying, "But I was an abused child and I overcame it, so he can, too," we are once again presuming that his reality is the same as ours. No two realities, no two people, no two lives, are ever the same. It is the greatest of human illusions to think that we are similar.

Experts tell us that drugs cause addicts to commit violence, but it is far more likely that, in many cases, the violence was there long before the drug problem, and who is to say how much violence a person might commit without drugs? We condescend and look down our noses at obese people, secretly judging them to be somehow inferior to ourselves, and yet we really have no idea just *why* it is they are overeating. Their reasons, thoughts, motives, emotions are not the same as ours, and instead of advising them to stop eating, we may perhaps commend them for making the better choice of the limited options available to them.

A smoker who gives up smoking may suffer a heart attack or stroke *after* giving up the habit because it was the cigarettes that enabled him to cope with a stressful life. A man who deserts his children may have beaten and abused them had he stayed. A woman who does not get the abortion she wanted may end up neglecting, abusing, or destroying her unwanted child.

In the last decade a lot of research has been done on perceptional differences and we now know that people are not only different in physical appearance, thoughts, emotions, and spirit, but they also perceive uniquely. What is deep red to one person is crimson to another, what is green to one is blue to another. People hear differently—some separate sounds, some cannot separate sounds, while still others hear certain sounds the rest of us never hear. We see uniquely. Some people focus on a single object, some focus on a wider range, while still others do not focus at all, but see the entire spectrum all at once. We presently call these "learning disabilities," but the truth is they are not disabilities at all, but merely everyone's different way of perceiving. Can we begin to imagine how differently each other's world is when we do not smell the same, touch the same, taste the same, or even see the same? We need to keep this in mind when we read another person's cards.

Divination may be defined as information relating to, or proceeding directly from God or a god; or as intuitive discovery. Our duty as cartomancers is to know that when we "divine," what we are receiving may be proceeding directly from God or a god, and on the other hand, what we are receiving could also be proceeding directly from our own subconscious. And what our subconscious whispers to us may be all right for us, but not necessarily for the other guy. Astute cartomancers realize they are mixing subconscious material with that from other sources. Whenever we fail to realize that we are imperfect instruments— that we can receive both accurate and inaccurate information— then we take the chance of forgetting what it is all about to begin with. This is why some psychics develop what is known as "Christ-consciousness," the condition where they believe themselves as unique and special hotlines to higher powers, forgetting that higher powers are within all of us, that not a single person is greater or lesser than another, that no one can say what is right or wrong for another.

Perhaps mankind's greatest sin is hubris—arrogance of the spirit—with which we not only believe we know what is best for the other fellow, but also believe we know what is best for God.

SELF-REALIZATION AND THE TAROT

If you decide to approach the tarot for your own self-realization, that is to say, from the viewpoint of individuation, you find that you will have completely different results than if you approach it with the purpose of improving others.

Jung believed that the problem of individuation was that the psyche consists of two incongruous halves. One half is conscious (the ego-consciousness), but the other half is unconscious, and as Jung states, ". . . unfortunately the unconscious really is unconscious; in other words, it is unknown." The task of the individual is to attempt to incorporate the two halves together to form a whole.[1]

Working with the tarot is not just a matter of freeing the unconscious, for if you free the unconscious but let go the conscious, you will find yourself in a bedlam of chaos. Denial of either the conscious or unconscious leads to madness, and the trick is to achieve a balance between the two so that your conscious serves your unconscious while at the same time your unconscious is serving your conscious.

In truth, all that exists in your environment is part of yourself. There is no one and nothing in your life that is not literally part of yourself. So it is that most people learn from outer experiences—where the outer unconscious part of the self comes

---

[1]C.G. Jung, *The Archetypes and the Collective Unconscious*, Bollingen Series XXX, translated by R.F.C. Hull (Princeton, NJ: Princeton University Press, 1959), p. 287.

in the form of others and outer events, so you eventually learn through the school of hard knocks. But the easier, faster, happier way to individuation happens when you *begin* with your unconscious, so that instead of having only physical events leading to inner growth, your inner unconscious leads you peacefully and lovingly to outer harmonious physical conditions. With this kind of growth from the inner to the outer, you become responsible for yourselves and magic happens in your lives, just like in the fairy tales.

In using tarot as an individualistic tool, if we look to ourselves for solutions to situations, without casting about for someone else to fulfill expectations or to be a scapegoat for our problems, we find in the cards the power to unleash the fullness of our latent potentiality. By trusting what the cards reveal through the unconscious, and then reasoning with the conscious, we can walk the road to self-transformation. Jung believed that all knowledge and strength derived from the individual and on the individual all the world depended.

> As at the beginning of the Christian Era, so again today we are faced with the problem of the moral backwardness which has failed to keep pace with our scientific, technical and social developments. So much is at stake and so much depends on the psychological constitution of modern man. Is he capable of resisting the temptation to use his power for the purpose of staging a world conflagration? Is he conscious of the path he is treading, and what the conclusions are that must be drawn from the present world situation and his own psychic situation? Does he know that he is on the point of losing the life-preserving myth of the inner man which Christianity has treasured up for him? Does he realize what lies in store should this catastrophe ever befall him? Is he even capable at all of realizing that this would be a catastrophe? And finally, does the individual know that *he* is the makeweight that tips the scales?

Happiness and contentment, equability of soul and meaningfulness of life—these can be experienced only by the individual and not by a State, which, on the one hand, is nothing but a convention of independent individuals and, on the other, continually threatens to paralyze and suppress the individual. . . . The social and political circumstances of the time are certainly of considerable significance, but their importance for the weal or woe of the individual has been boundlessly overestimated in so far as they are taken for the sole deciding factors. In this respect all our social goals commit the error of overlooking the psychology of the person for whom they are intended and—very often—of promoting only his illusions.

. . . I am neither spurred on by excessive optimism nor in love with high ideals, but am merely concerned with the fate of the individual human being—that infinitesimal unit on whom a world depends, and in whom, if we read the meaning of the Christian message aright, even God seeks his goal![2]

Jung suggests that not only is all of life about the individual, as indeed, we each experience life as private single units, but also suggests that it is to the individual that we must look for the hope of the human race. It would seem that if it is our destiny to help others, we can do this best by helping ourselves.

Each of us is a container of God's perceptions. It has been intimated that perhaps God is lonely and that is why life exists. If we will not be the individual containers of God's perceptions where then will It put Its perceptions? There is no greater, nor more difficult, task than to know one's self, which is why we so naturally choose to take the easy road of looking at others instead of ourselves, but *for one single individual to truly transform*

---

[2]C.G. Jung, *The Undiscovered Self* (New York: Mentor Books, 1958), pp. 123–125.

himself or herself is to change the universe. If we can make of ourselves a joyful container for God's perceptions, then it might just be that we shall discover not only ourselves, but also others, and in the process, even God.

Each of us has the means to be a complete total package within ourselves, yet so few are able. To become whole is such an unfathomable task that it not only eludes us, but many are not even aware such a state can exist. We can use the tarot as a means to bring some portion of that awareness to our attention. And once we have *truly* become one with anything, once we become aware of anything's *being* so that it is also our being, it is ours to keep for eternity, our's to add to in successive steps up the spiraling ladder of consciousness, never to be taken from us. Anything we truly become aware of in spirit, heart, mind, and body is ours to keep because by becoming part of it, we have become another part of The Whole, and The Whole can never be taken from Itself.

CHAPTER 4

Divination

*E*verything in the tarot—suits, numbers, titles, colors, court cards—all are symbols of the archetypes. The archetypes are processes of like-motion, which, from our viewpoint makes them appear to constantly flow into different patterns of perception. Like motion, they are forever interchangeable and non-specific, and this makes them impossible to define. Because of this evasiveness, people have always attempted to express essence with symbols.

The Major Arcana are a symbolic representation of twenty-two archetypal forces. In a reading, they show us what major forces are active in our lives at that specific time. They are immense and often unseen, but they form the network for all that will come to manifest in our realities.

The Minor Arcana shows us the event or situation that will take place as the archetype interpenetrates time-space. The Minor Arcana enables us to see how the Major Arcana are being played out in our daily actions and day-to-day choices. It is from the Minor that we can see our most mundane earth living, and because of this, it is an exciting part of the tarot.

In the court cards, we see the behavioral patterns. The court cards tell us about certain personality types and the special ways different people perceive reality. They show us human traits and characteristics found in groupings of individuals.

The four suits are the four phases to success of anything. They are the four phases of energy—the correct playing out of

energy to achieve success by universal law. All processes involve
these four steps if the success of anything is to be accomplished
and when you skip any one of these steps, you miss the objec-
tive. The spiritual goal is to become aware of these four processes
within yourself so you can create a completely balanced man-
dala of yourself. In so doing, by becoming aware of a part, you
become aware of The Whole, in exact proportion to your awareness of self.

The numbers are the patterns that the archetypes weave.
The different groupings of the numbers indicate some of the
diverse ways that archetypes arrange themselves in your life. An
archetype is never static. It is in constant motion, forming and
creating new patterns and re-structuring old ones. This is called
the dance of the archetypes.

The pictures, colors, and arrangements depicted on tarot
cards are attempts by different people to express through symbols their personal interpretations of how they see the archetypes. Because archetypes, insofar as we are able to discern
them, originate from the collective unconscious, even though
different artists and authors will color the archetypes to a
greater or lesser extent with their own personal realities and
interpretations, the archetypes will still maintain to a great
degree their own autonomy and purity derived from their collective universality.

If we do not limit our interpretations of these symbols we
allow ourselves to open up and expand to possibilities hitherto
unbeknownst to us. One of the greatest dangers for new card
readers is to limit the possible interpretations. It is human
nature to want to categorize all things into convenient slots so
that we can identify and define them. This is all right, as long as
we keep in mind that each categorization is only *one* definition
of a multitude. It is not all, nor even most of it. It is only a tiny
part that is colored (and often violated) by our own personal
beliefs and attitudes.

Sometimes when you do a reading the cards will not seem to
answer what you ask. At first, you may think you have done

something wrong, so you lay out the cards again. Once more, they appear to have missed your point – it's like you want to talk about apples, but the cards insist on talking about oranges. Don't be misled into thinking that you are not communicating or that you are not doing something correctly. When this happens, the cards are sometimes trying to communicate a very important unknown message. You do not control the archetypes, and they do not control you. They are using you as a channel. If you do not like what they are saying, or if they refuse to address your question, it may be that they are trying to communicate something of much greater value at this time. Or sometimes you just don't understand everything that is involved in the issue. What may appear to be so clear to you as one thing may turn out to be something quite different in the future.

Perhaps a person reading the cards wants to know more about his marriage. Maybe he is worried because his spouse seems unattentive as of late. He's emotionally upset, and he wants to know through the cards if his spouse still loves him, if his marriage is in trouble. Maybe he's having questions himself about how he feels concerning his marriage. Laying out the cards, he expects to receive an abundance of cups, but instead he receives all discs and one wand. Befuddled, he picks up the cards, shuffles them, and lays them out again. Once more, the cards are discs and maybe this time one cup. "What does that have to do with the price of eggs?" he asks. Maybe the only thing he feels is right about the relationship at this particular time is the physical part, so how in this world do all these discs tell him anything? It may be so tempting not to trust the cards. But hopefully he will remember they see what is not visible, and what is visible is not seen. If he makes the mistake of clinging to his ego to control the flow of events, or if he twists the cards' meanings to suit his own wishes, he runs the risk of blocking creative energy, thus the truth of the matter. He will miss what may be very vital and real. It may just be that six weeks down the road, or three months down the road, he is going to find himself in an almost completely disc situation with this relationship that will change or lay to waste most of what he deemed important in it up until then. Perhaps there is a totally unexpected child entering the relationship that will ground both he and his spouse up to their necks in earthbound living (and discs) and will make insignificant to him any emotional problems he may have thought he had before. The cards usually address what they know to be important, knowing ahead of time that what we are worried about is sometimes not the crux of the issue at all.

We can know but little under the best of circumstances. We may pride ourselves on our accuracy with the cards so that after a while we begin to think that we've got the hot scoop. But to think we are wise is folly. In truth, the more we know, the more we know we don't know. Answers are seldom either/or; more often, the answers are "all of the above." C.J. Cirlot in *The Dictionary of Symbols* says:

. . . in all the examples of deformation of symbols one finds the same basic falsification: The creative drive of the symbol—its tendency to revert to its Origin—is restricted, and it is made to bear labels which are over-concrete, too materialized or inferior. Its metaphysical function is arrested, and consequently, a single plane of reality comes to be mistaken for the sum of all possible levels of symbolic meaning.

. . . The influence of the symbol must be allowed to pervade all levels of reality; only then can it be seen in all its spiritual grandeur and fecundity . . . .

The symbolic object appears as a quality or a higher form, and also as an essence justifying and explaining the existence of the symbolizing agent. The most straightforward of symbological analyses based upon simple enumeration of the qualitative meanings of the object, sometimes, while the "mode of existence" is being investigated, will reveal a sudden opening which illuminates its meaning through an association of ideas. This association should never be thought of as a mere external idea in the mind of the investigator, outside the symbol itself, but rather as a revelation of the inner link—the "common rhythm"—joining two realities to the mutual benefit of both.[1]

Because archetypes are groupings of like-energy as created and derived from the Source, they follow, as does all energy, certain universal laws as established by the likeness of their natures. As mysterious and omnipotent as archetypes are in their motion, it is these very universal laws that make it possible for us to predict directions they may take.

The tendency or necessity of an archetype to unite or reconcile with matrices of its own like code-pattern is the basis of divination in tarot. It is this archetypal law that causes not only tarot, but all of life, to re-create itself out of itself. It is also well worth noting that if energy is attracted to its likeness, it similarly is repelled from its opposition. Like a magnet it will attract or oppose, forming either thesis or antithesis, depending upon its origin, structure, and dynamics.

Another universal tendency is that an archetype, if broken or damaged, will attempt to come back together to re-form its original symmetry. Being a centrical process, when disrupted it will strive to regain its totality as a complete code-pattern. An archetype will always attempt to balance and complete itself. There is no such thing as an accident or chance, and what we perceive as an accident or luck is nothing other than an archetype forming its symmetry. All of life is destiny and fate— archetypes coming together to complete themselves.

The necessity of an archetype to unite with its own like code-pattern and its tendency to come back together again

---

[1]J.E. Cirlot, *A Dictionary of Symbols* (New York: Philosophical Library, 1971), pp. 1, li, lii.

when damaged are both examples of the same universal law. Like-Attracts-Like.

Let's say we know a man named Sam. Sam is what we would call a bad driver. He drives too fast, he tailgates, and he is an offensive rather than a defensive driver. Naturally, Sam thinks he's an excellent driver and prides himself on the fact that he has never had an accident that was "my fault." But Sam has the archetype of offensive driving, so he will draw accidents to himself. There is no such thing as an innocent party when viewed from a higher level. Sam will draw accidents to him by other people who are completing their offensive driving archetypes or who possess some compatible blueprint that resonates in some part of its like code-pattern with Sam's. Sometimes it will appear to be one person's fault and sometimes another person's fault, but always in some way it will be the symmetries of *both* parties because they are completing and balancing each other.

Of course, this is greatly simplified, and there are many different processes at work in each case. Sam's case provides a grossly understated hypothetical example. It is hopelessly simplistic to just say that offensive driving symmetries are drawn together, for one cannot possibly know all the forces involved in any case. Two people can come together for what appears to be entirely different reasons, and from our human viewpoint, the archetypes they are completing can hardly be guessed. In the case of Sam's bad driving, the other driver involved may drive offensively for completely different reasons. Perhaps Sam drives badly because he feels inferior, inadequate, and driving offensively gives him a feeling of power. Maybe the other driver drives offensively because he is unhappy, or has a death wish because of something in his psyche or life he finds unbearable. We cannot really know the underlying, unseen forces at work, but we can say that driving offensively brought them together to complete a symmetry which they both compelled upon themselves.

Archetypes follow the universal law of completion because they are always attracted to their own likenesses. We have debated about destiny and fate for centuries, right along with the issue of free will. Destiny—fate—free will—are all different words for the same universal law of Like-Attracts-Like. Our *destinies* (*destinations*) are *determined* by our unconscious *desires*, or by what we are like. Our free will is our freedom to determine what we are like. The confusion lies in that we insist on believing that free will means we can get what we want, or what we like. The truth of the matter is that we do not get what we like, but rather, we get what we *are* like.

It has been hotly debated certainly more than once that if people get what they are like, how is it that something bad can happen to a young child, who is completely innocent? How could a child possibly draw a negative event? If like can only attract like, it does not seem plausible in the case of a child that anything bad should happen to it, yet we all know that accidents, mishaps, and bad luck happen all the time to children and innocents.

Only knowledge, acceptance, and understanding of all levels can help to comprehend this at its extremely painful physical level, and when it comes to pain and suffering, we are unfortunately stuck at this physical level. If we cannot understand grief with our hearts, we can sometimes understand it intellectually, however.

Just because a child has only recently entered Earth living does not necessarily make its soul young. Given the eons of eternity, who is to say who is the younger or older soul on Earth—the child or the old man? Age cannot be measured in Earth years, for a single entire lifetime is but as a sudden flash of light as measured by the infinitude of our spirits. Even though adults may appear to be older, in truth some infants are far, far older than their parents.

Also, there may be truth to the old adage that only the good die young. It is we the living who remain behind that suffer anguish at the death of a loved one, not necessarily the dead. If we could but know what awaits the soul of a loved one in its next re-birth into the Light we would perhaps dance with joy when those we love go on.

And finally, death and suffering are difficult to comprehend and accept from our human eyes. That does not mean that they are bad. It has been said that it is Earth living that is the most difficult of all, and perhaps it is only because we cannot see further that we call bad what we cannot understand. It is a fact, however sad and torturous it sounds, that some of the wisest and most wondrous people of all are those who have suffered the most, and who is to say what beauty they have gained that we cannot even begin to guess at, and what their final reward will be?

• • •

Our fundamental beliefs are the basis of all thought, emotion, and matter that are present in our lives, so that material realizations are simply the manifestation of archetypes produced by our beliefs. It is unconscious belief that attracts the archetype, that is eventually displayed (or manifested) in time-space. It is a mistake to think that only what we *consciously* think and believe will come to pass. It is our *unconscious* belief that forms our reality—not conscious thought. Sometimes thoughts are the same as beliefs, but just as often they are not.

What we hold in our unconscious will, in some way, express itself physically. Physical and spiritual, mental and emotional will merge, becoming two sides of a single coin. An archetype will erupt where it feels the most pressure and where it exerts the strongest hold. A great deal of its existence is on other planes, and to repress or to be ignorant of what it is merely increases its power to complete itself on the physical plane. If we do not allow it to complete itself by unfoldment on an inner level, it will attempt to complete itself on the outer—through other people and outer events in our lives. Either way it will come home to roost because it must.

This is how divination works—by the simple, yet profoundly neglected, denied, and misunderstood universal law of Like-Attracts-Like. Every single thing in the Universe, without exception, must go to its own likeness. Literally every single spirit, being, emotion and thought must be born out of itself, live from itself, and die unto itself, for archetypes are harmonically resonant. The Universe is absolute order because order is harmony and harmony is God. The Universe is uni-verse, one verse, one song.

Once we grasp this, we wonder how we managed to miss it all along. It is how an egg and a sperm come together; how for millennia the same embryos have been formed over and over again in each species, each after its own kind; how all forms are created in their own likenesses. Indeed, how God creates human beings in Its own image. It is how for untold generations birds have managed to fly thousands of miles to their same ancestral destinations; why the solar systems are created and destroyed and held together in their circular cycles; why male and female are drawn together; and why crystals and snowflakes are six-sided. It is the rise and fall of the stock market, the atom bomb, the war between Iran and Iraq, the war between Israel and Palastine, all wars; it is the rain becoming rivers, becoming humidity, becoming clouds, becoming rain; it is addictions, depression, anger, and grief; it is the seasons, the continents and the oceans, the hot and the cold. It is the regularly repeating internal arrangement of atoms in like objects, both material and non-material, found everywhere in everything in the entire Universe. All is balance maintaining balance by the eternal universal law of like attracting like. Virtually everything in the Universe forms itself out of itself, so that constant creation, destruction, and re-structuring are taking place according to what exists.

In divination, when we concentrate and lay out the cards, the layout will attempt to complete itself. It will integrate the forces involved in itself. It doesn't matter if we aren't aware of its presence in our selves and in our lives because the archetype's existence doesn't depend on our conscious perception of it.

With the cards we are taking seventy-eight archetypal symbols and laying them out to form their own patterns. If we concentrate, accept, and work with the cards long enough, our own symmetry will form with that of the cards, and in them we may perceive the behavior of that which we wish to know. It is a natural law that works with or without our conscious knowledge, belief, or approval of it.

Before we can expect balance from the cards, though, we must first have balance within ourselves, for we will draw our own reflections from the deck. We need to accept both our physical and psychic environment without excluding one or the other. To concentrate solely on the psyche or solely on the physical results in rigid thought patterns will not let us harmonize with the Universe.

When you are interpreting the cards, you are listening to the conscious, the subconscious, and the superconscious. If you reach a certain degree of awareness, when doing a reading you will perceive the Force flowing from the archetypes to you, from you to the person being read for, from the person being read for back to you, and around again. You will understand that all you see as reality is only illusion and only as each of us perceives it. It's like trying to describe the entire elephant by only perceiving its toe. If done correctly, divining can be a painful process, and certainly not one easily undergone, because you are acutely aware that you are only perceiving the elephant's toe, and what's worse, you are just as aware that the possibility of making your client perceive that as well might be difficult!

The cards are meant to be used for divination but your readings may not be accurate. The cards are only as accurate as what the diviner sees and what the hearer hears. Thoughts are things, so you will see what you think you see because you see only what you look at and hear only what you listen to, and thus, it will come to pass. You will not see nor hear what will not come to pass because you do not perceive it. And if you don't perceive it, how can it be for you?

Symbols in the tarot can help you understand archetypal behavior, your self, and how life functions. The tarot, if used properly, teaches you to think vertically and not just horizontally. As Cirlot suggests, while the average person is cognizant of relationships only between horizontal groups of being, the mystic sees vertical bridges between those objects which are within the same cosmic rhythm. Thus, higher and lower and the most seemingly disparate phenomena are brought together and seen through the scynchronicities of their common tendencies. "Symbolism is what might be called a magnetic force, drawing together phenomena which have the same rhythm and even allowing them to interchange."[2] When we study the tarot, we study the Gods and Goddesses, ourselves, life, other people, and all things that have consciousness. It is a never ending process.

---

[2]Cirlot, *A Dictionary of Symbols*, p. xxxiii.

CHAPTER 5

Choosing Your Deck

All of us are drawn to the tarot for different reasons. Some accidentally pick up a book and start reading it. Some are persuaded by a friend to go for a reading "just for the fun of it." Others are led to it from other esoteric study because it's natural to expand outward to similar fields as we grow and learn. There are those who stumble onto it by seeing a tarot deck at a friend's house or in a shop. Idle curiosity may bring us to pick up a deck, and from that moment we are hooked. But one way or the other, tarot finds us if we are ready to be found. There is something about a tarot deck that immediately engulfs us with sensations of *déjà vu* when we are ready to begin on its journey. It is an eerie feeling, often a strangely familiar one, picking up that first tarot deck that is yours.

Because every person is a special and unique individual we all will respond differently to various decks. Sometimes there is that magical moment of immediate recognition when we happen to spot a deck for the first time, like remembering an old friend that we weren't aware we had forgotten, and we feel so happy to see it again. It's like, "Where have you been all my life?" Others are not so sure, and it is more like meeting a new friend for the first time, and it isn't until we have worked with the cards for awhile that our newfound friendship with a certain deck finally begins to develop. And then there are the multifarious among us who like a number of decks, enjoying the unique variations that each deck has to offer according to our mood of the moment. One talented cartomancer uses thirteen decks! Searching for the right deck is loads of fun because there are so many excellent decks to choose from now. Even if you end up only choosing one or two decks, it is still an exciting education to study and get to know all the different decks available.

The cards themselves are not the actual Light-blueprint archetypes any more than we are. We both are simply material manifestations of higher forms. The actual images on the cards are physical representations of the archetypes which are interpenetrating on all levels. When choosing a deck, if you just go with your intuition you will probably end up with the right deck because that emotion of being drawn to, liking, or feeling comfortable with a certain deck is your unconscious drawing together like-symmetries—yours and the deck's. If you can start trusting your intuition from the very start, and later add to it with knowledge, feeling, and actual physical practice, you soon find that your unconscious knew right from the very beginning what your conscious wasn't so sure of.

One of the best ways to express true archetypal resonance is through color because color impacts the unconscious with a subtle force all its own. Unfortunately, those of us who are consciously aware of being affected by color will have difficulty with most decks that are on the market today. I mention color because color *is* important. Whereas there are many fine decks available in an array of design, symbol, and trait that correspond quite nicely with the archetype being featured, for some strange reason, most artists of tarot decks seem to be unaware of the importance of color. A color is an archetype, too, and to paint an archetypal image in an incorrect color or with the incorrect color of background can create disaster in the subconscious mind when it comes to divining. It is important that the numbers, elements, symbols, *and* colors all resonate as a total harmonic whole on every card, so that the card can be employed as a complete instrument to freely connect with your higher consciousness.

There are a few decks, however, that have miraculously achieved this total picture, including color. *The Motherpeace Deck* by Karen Vogel and Vicki Noble[1] is not only exceptional in its correct color correspondences, but is also extremely unique because it is one of the very few decks that successfully deploys people for archetypal images in its Minor Arcana. Somehow Vogel and Noble have managed to catch the essence of the archetypes in the very simplest of motion and form, using people as the symbol of both action and reaction, cause and effect. This deck is a soft and gentle representation of archetypes, making it a joy to work with for those of us who have trouble digesting images like nine swords protruding out of a bloody corpse.

Another deck that employs the correct color correspondences (and with an accuracy that is downright uncanny) is the *Thoth Deck* by Aleister Crowley and Lady Freida Harris.[2] Whatever one may think of Crowley, and opinions do vary, his deck is still considered a masterpiece of tarot by most authorities. Another comment about both *Motherpeace* and *Thoth*—both decks are unique in that all three sections have been done well— the Major, the Minor, and the court cards. It is easy to find decks that are well done in one or two areas. In the *Thoth* and *Motherpeace* decks, however, all three sections are expertly represented, presenting an outstanding combination of balanced polarities for both the conscious and unconscious mind to work with.

The Yeager Tarot of Meditation by Marty Yeager[3] is interesting because it has an absolutely magnificent Major Arcana. The Major Arcana is also well done in the *Barbara Walker Tarot* deck.[4] Both Yeager and Walker have modernized the Major

---

[1]Karen Vogel and Vicki Noble, *Motherpeace Round Tarot Deck* (Stamford, CT: U.S. Games, 1983).

[2]Aleister Crowley and Lady Frieda Harris, *Thoth Tarot Deck* (Stamford, CT: U.S. Games, and York Beach, ME: Samuel Weiser, 1977).

[3]Marty Yeager, *Yeager Tarot of Meditation* (Stamford, CT: U.S. Games, 1982).

[4]Barbara Walker, *Barbara Walker Tarot* (Stamford, CT: U.S. Games, 1986).

Arcana while maintaining its traditional meanings. This is important because the traditional interpretations are still, in their own way, the truest of forms.

There are many fine decks,[5] but be careful, because there are some who have apparently not only missed the mark with color, but also in their pictorial representations by presenting only one side of a two-sided coin. An archetype is whole—not entirely bad nor entirely good—it is a yin-yang of wholeness, and some artists of tarot decks dwell on only one half of its totality. It takes a great deal of both psychic and mystic knowledge, combined with inner harmony, to be able to know and then paint in physical form the corresponding vibrations of suit, number, color, positivity, negativity, and symbols of any one archetype, much less seventy-eight of them! As cartomancers, we rely on our cards to help provide this knowledge to us, so it is of utmost importance that we choose a deck created by someone who has an abundance of knowledge and wisdom of the one-ness of all things.

While we're discussing picking out the right deck, let's not overlook playing cards. Some people feel a natural innate kinship with common playing cards and if you feel drawn to them, they can be used to divine quite successfully, sometimes even better than with a tarot deck. If you want to use playing cards, plus still maintain the benefits of having the Major Arcana, it's fun to choose your favorite Major Arcana from a tarot deck, cut it down to size so that it will shuffle easily with playing cards, and make your own tarot deck so you can use both sets of symbols.

After bringing the cards home, they should be studied, held, and made to be your current focal point of interest. Get acquainted, become familiar with them and get to know them as you would a new friend. Place them in a container that they feel

---

[5]Any of the decks mentioned in this chapter and many others may be purchased from Samuel Weiser, Box 612, York Beach, ME 03910, if your local bookstore doesn't carry them.

at "home" in, such as a bag, pouch, chest, box, basket, or case, or simply wrap them in a silk scarf. A small chest or case is good, or any container made of natural elements, such as wood, glass, cardboard, or woven straw. A wooden box or glass case is attractive and it protects the cards from possible bending or damage. It can be terribly upsetting to lose your cards because the dog likes to chew cardboard boxes or because of a spilled soda. If you use a bag or pouch it should be made of silk, cotton, rayon (rayon is made from the pulp of a tree), wool, or any completely natural fiber, *except leather.*

As opposed to a case, a bag has the advantage of being pliable enough to fit nicely into a purse or pocket. You might enjoy making your own, in which case you can use any kind of attractive outer cloth and then line it with silk or another natural fiber, so that the cards themselves will be surrounded only by natural elements. The fun part of any of these—bag, box, or case—is that they can be decorated any way you wish. Some people like to place a crystal of some sort in the container with their cards, or enjoy designing their favorite symbols on a bag, or attaching a favorite amulet or piece to the drawstring.

It's generally not a good idea to let other people handle the cards that you are using for your own personal readings. Many cartomancers keep a personal deck that they use only for themselves, and use separate decks when reading for other people. Keeping your own personal deck away from the vibrations of others makes it easier for you and the cards to keep the energy pure and just between the two of you. After a while you will develop a close working relationship with the deck, one that flows easily and smoothly from the resonances of your undisturbed rhythms working together without the interference of archetypes that may have been drawn in from other people's energy. But in all matters of the cards, you should do what feels most comfortable to you. What works for someone else may not necessarily work for you, and it is important to do what comes naturally and forthright.

All material forms need to be kept in touch with the four elements, which is why our furniture peels and cracks when it gets too dry and why our bodies need heat and light from the sun to survive. Now and then we may find that our card readings are getting kind of fuzzy or becoming just downright inaccurate, and when this happens it may indicate that the cards are in need of balance. Watch this closely because when the cards are out of balance it's usually a signal that we are, too. There is nothing in the environment that is not part of us, and when something as close to us as our cards begins showing a need for clarity it's a waving flag of like attracting like. One reason card readings may become inaccurate or cloudy is because our cards have gotten out of balance by being out of contact with all four elements. Sitting in a pouch over a period of time tends to rob them of some of their elemental vibrations, just like what happens when we neglect to exercise, eat right, or stretch our intuitive instincts because we have been stagnating in an office or living in a rut. When this happens, it's time to revitalize our cards by re-establishing their contact with the four elements (fire, water, air and earth). Of course, it would be much better to keep the cards continually in balance by having a regular routine of purification, rather than having to be told by them to get on the stick, but often we treat our cards like we treat ourselves, forgetting that "an ounce of prevention is worth a pound of cure."

The element earth can be absorbed by the cards by putting them on a pan of dirt, in the pot of a large plant, or on a natural rock large enough to hold them. There are some beautiful crystal formations and large single stones available at rock shops and these can hold the cards to revitalize them.

To soak up water and air, you can use air particles laden with moisture by placing the cards on the rim of a cup of water that has been placed on a windowsill on a humid day. Nights are good for this, too, because the dew from the cool night air is particularly wet, plus it never hurts to soak up a few receptive moonbeams.

For fire, the deck can be placed in sunshine or passed repeatedly over burning incense or the flame and smoke from a lighted candle.

You can think of your own ways to get both you and your cards back in balance, as a little fresh air doesn't hurt us either, keeping in mind that the more natural these four elements are, the better restored you both will be. The more frequently and longer you and your cards are kept in touch with the four elements, the clearer you will remain.

In working with the cards, if you are persistent and insistent you will eventually be rewarded with proficiency. As Aleister Crowley once said, "Persistence is the only quality required for success." Given time, experience, and determination, a successful relationship can develop between the cards and the reader that will last a lifetime. Because archetypes create more of themselves out of themselves, or put another way, because likeness can only attract more of itself, the proficient accuracy of a truly honest and loving cartomancer can only increase in time, and the relationship between you and your cards will grow more and more dependable. The cards themselves reveal a perfect system of life, and once truly understood, the cards reveal many astonishing things about your life.

CHAPTER 6

An Introduction to the Cards

Each part of the tarot deck expresses a segment of necessary symmetries working on this planet. Each section of a deck of cards can be broken down to show a certain aspect or action of the archetypes, and thus, to show us our own lives. There is no part of the deck that is not an integral key to the functioning and patterns of our own lives. These sections, or overlays of patterns, are all seen to be indigenous to any process, and to have even one of them missing would be rather like a team of horses without their carriage, a cake without eggs and salt, or a typewriter with half its keys. For although the tarot is only a particle of the universe in itself, it is unique in that it is a representation of many particles within the one. That is what makes it so extremely flexuous and circuitous, much like a laby-rinth. This labyrinth has sections that overlay and intertwine to form one complete archetype from its seventy-eight separate parts. The six sections that make up the tarot are the Major Arcana, Minor Arcana, court cards, four suits, numbers, and colors.

THE MAJOR ARCANA

The Major Arcana consists of twenty–two images of arche-types that are present in the human world. The major arche-types have been called gods, angels, fallen angels, demons, dev-ils, spirits, ghosts, saviors, the higher self, and, of course, archetypes. Their presence has always been felt in one way or another, and even the most obstinate fundamentalist will know about them because the Major Arcana symbolizes the forms of the subconscious, conscious, and superconscious, all-pervading in the hearts and souls of all people everywhere, and whether the fundamentalist realizes it or not, it is from these archetypes that people derive their destiny.

THE MINOR ARCANA

The Minor Arcana represents how we specifically experience the Major because the Minor functions in the steps of the Major. It's the codes of the Light blueprint one level closer to materialization. More simply stated, the Minor Arcana symbolises mundane events and situations that occur in our daily lives. Scholars who do not understand the totality of the tarot claim that the Minor is the stepchild of the Major and that occultists really don't know what to do with it. Only those who haven't explored the Minor in any depth could begin to say such a thing. The Minor Arcana is the expression of the archetypes through human activities, the physical manifestation of essence through events, the playing out of the Major archetypes through to the physical plane. It represents code-principles spiraling through to express and manifest themselves in patterns of events and activities corresponding to like-motions as viewed by our physical angle. Certainly it is the most exciting part of the tarot from a mundane viewpoint in that it is from the Minor that we can see and identify events that are going to actually occur in our lives. Sometimes when doing the cards we fail to see this because we forget that the physical plane is not only material manifestation, but also emotional and mental manifestation. For instance, the Ace of Discs indicates the beginning of something materially new, while the Ace of Cups means the beginning of something emotionally new.

THE COURT CARDS

In the court cards we see people themselves. Court cards do not represent actual events or situations as the Minor Arcana does—they are the human actors in an archetypal world of light and darkness. The court cards are the archetypes interweaving with the matrices of people, carrying the origin, structure, and dynamics of their own particular conciliating arrangement, each according to its own matrix-code, ultimately manifesting in some sort of human behavior. Through the court cards we see behavior patterns, the personality types that make up the human race, people's modes of perceiving their world, and how people filter the presence of all that is around them into their own lives. The court cards tell us of personalities, traits, and habits. When it comes to understanding, it is the court cards that are the most difficult to comprehend. The court cards are sixteen different psychological types and they show us how each of these uniquely perceives his or her environment. How we perceive things determines how we will act, what will motivate and drive us, and how we respond and react to our world.

THE FOUR SUITS

The four suits are the four steps in the process that all consciousness on the physical plane must proceed through in order to obtain success in anything. If any one of these four steps is missed in any process, then the success of that process is not achieved. The four suits are a necessary playing out of energy as set up on Earth. The importance of the four suits cannot be overemphasized. There are four elements, four seasons, four directions, four points to a cross, four steps in meditation, four levels in the Qaballah, and many more, as will be explained in chapter 6, because four steps are necessary to achieve *anything*. These four steps are (1) getting the energy together so it can begin; (2) utilizing the energy; (3) nurturing the energy; (4)

ordering up the energy. In meditation, they are (1) purification, (2) concentration, (3) insight, (4) transformation. The Qaballah describes these same four steps as (1) origination, (2) creation, (3) formation, and (4) expression. There is nothing that we can think of that does not require these four steps in order to succeed or to achieve completion. When we lack knowledge of these four steps we easily become confused, yet it's human nature to try to go from the first to the fourth without incorporating the missed steps. Then there is no completion, only pain or confusion. Sometimes we skip certain steps because we are ignorant of them, but most times the step(s) that we end up skipping are the ones that are actually missing in ourselves.

THE NUMBERS

The numbers are the "dances of the archetypes." The numbers are the ways that archetypes play out their many sequences and coagencies, which is why numbers are seen to be infinite and magical. As with numbers in anything, the inexhaustible variety of dances stretches out to eternity, but because all primal patterns are comprised of the one Whole, if only the primary numbers 1 through 10 are learned and absorbed, you can catch the basic rhythm of all rhythms. Numbers are perfect examples of archetypes reaching out and feeding back into themselves, creating spirals and mandalas that continually explode and implode, structure and re-structure, create and destroy, out of their one basic unity. In numbers can be seen cycles, endlessly repeating themselves with external arrangements differing according to the internal ordering of the symmetries at the present time and the nature of the archetypes themselves.

COLORS

Colors are also archetypes. Colors are not to be thought of as symbols representing archetypes, but as actually being archetypes themselves. The Source sends forth its code-principles via light, sound, and color according to our perceptions. As with all archetypes, these are perceived differently according to your capabilities at each level. At the Earth level, when you see the color purple in an object it is actually the color yellow that has interpenetrated the substance, for the human eye perceives the opposite end of the color spectrum. Color is an arrangement of energy-motion, like sound and light, and it remains a non-linear gridwork even after interpenetrating Earth consciousness. Color is the essence of the archetype, which shows its impact, its nature.

REVIEW

The following list sums up the various components that you need to consider when reading the cards:

1) Major Arcana—the pure energy of the archetypes before or as they enter the earth plane. The actual energy that will be experienced.

2) Minor Arcana—how the energies of the Major Arcana are expressed through actual physical events and situations.

3) Court Cards—the sixteen types of people or types of human behavior.

4) Four Suits—the four steps that 1) take in energy, 2) utilize energy, 3) nurture energy, 4) order up energy.

5) Numbers—the different combinations of energy available; how the energy or situation arranges itself to play out.

6) Colors—the nature of the energy or its impact and force on the physical, i.e., red is dynamic and force-

ful, blue is peaceful and comforting, pink is soft and
giving.

The tarot is a masterpiece of archetypal symbols, but archetypes are not just the hidden twenty-two Major energies, the
forty Minor activities, the four suit steps, the sixteen types of
people, the cycles of the numbers, and the forceful impact of the
colors—archetypes are everything. For archetypes are not entities, but processes. Archetypes are arrangements of motion,
energy, all of life. How lucky we are to have the tarot—a real and
viable narrowing down of the infinitude of archetypes to
seventy-eight that the mind can easily deal with.

It is not to be assumed that the tarot, as it is, represents
completion any more than playing cards represent completion.
The entire cosmos is in a constant state of creation, learning
itself, living itself, loving itself. Whenever you embark upon
something, it is a source of interest and you are studying only a
part of the whole. And yet, like the tarot, if you learn the part
you are also, by necessity, learning the whole. Knowledge of the
gods is imperfect and incomplete, and we are fortunate indeed
to have what little knowledge we do. And we are also blessed by
its very simplicity because as Carl G. Jung said, "The entire
universe is found in the smallest of particles which therefore
corresponds to the whole."[1]

So if we take any *one* thing in our lives and learn that one
thing as completely and thoroughly as we can, we are in effect
learning the essence of it all. It doesn't matter what activity or
tool we choose—whether it be the tarot or playing cards, music,
anatomy, walking, or bouncing a ball. If we take any activity,
art, or skill—no matter how seemingly trivial—as far as we can
take it, and push it to the limits, to its extreme, as far as we and
it can go together, and push it beyond where we and it have ever
been before, then we find ourselves propelled from complexity
into utter simplicity. But we must pursue it beyond both for if

---

[1]C.G. Jung, *Psyche and Symbol* (Garden City, NY: Doubleday Anchor, 1958), p. 250.

we stop at ourselves we have learned neither it, nor another, nor much of anything else. But if taken on and on until that one utter fantastic moment—we will suddenly discover there is no separation between it, ourselves, or anything else.

The tarot is one of the most transcending prototypes of this. For by its very nature it is attempting to express our relationship with The All, the cosmos, consciousness, and with our species. The tarot is as limited or unlimited as we are. It can carry us to the extremes of our center and circumference, and as it does, it will carry itself with us.

When your first tarot deck calls, you are ready to enter the realm of the High Priestess. By listening to the inner voices, what is inside will become outside and what is outside will become inside. And if you pursue her path with all your might and sincerity and perserverence, you may someday find that the High Priestess is but one of many paths, all leading to no where because you are already there.

CHAPTER 7

The Numbers

The first four numbers, 1 through 4, represent the four suits, four elements, the four phases, the four psychological functions, the four points, four phases of the moon, the four seasons, etc. Four is the number of processing on the physical plane, and even though the form that four takes is different, its successive motion never changes. In all that is around us—be it getting up in the morning, going to a ball game, or to visit Aunt Nellie—all forms have these four steps of motion. When we get up in the morning, we more or less 1) finish taking in energy. We struggle between being awake and asleep, finishing up our sleep as we begin to awaken. 2) We utilize energy; we finally get up and get going. 3) We nurture energy—have a cup of coffee, wash our faces, get dressed. 4) We order up energy and begin the day's chores, the day's productivity.

To learn the numbers it helps to lay the cards out day after day to watch how they play out. See if the 9 of Swords is positive—perhaps reaching a mental conclusion, or negative—experiencing depression. What it means to one person will not necessarily work for another. Also, the meaning will change from time to time and the same person will experience a 9 of Swords as solving a mental problem one time, and indicating mental turmoil at another. As the situation or person changes, so will the card.

Having said this, it is rather fascinating, however, to watch the processes of the numbers in our lives because it is incredible how often the number or card will have the same meaning over and over again, regardless of how situations may seem different each time. This probably indicates that the cards change only as we do, and sometimes we are not changing nearly as much as we think we are. Studying and analyzing numbers and cards to see if they change and how they play out can bring deep insight into personality and individual growth. You can work with the following keywords and definitions of numbers:

1
An Origination. Conceiving.
Conception. Seed. The beginning. Gifts. You are going to have to do something! Yourself. Taking in energy.

The Ace is the unmanifested beginning. It has not yet begun on any physical level that can be recognized, and it may or may not be recognized in the conscious mind, as it is a process of rising from the unconscious. The Ace indicates that the conception is taking place on the inner, but it will not be visible until the 2. It is the seed, but the tree has not yet sprouted. When you get an Ace, even though you may not yet be consciously aware of it, you are going to have to do something! Many times the Ace is a gift. It may appear as a gift from others or as a gift from the inner that we are going to help give ourselves.

2
A Creation. Utilizing.
Unfolding. Being together, going together, working together. All pairs of wholes, which may appear as opposites. Yourself and the other. Putting energy to work.

The 2 is where the Ace sprouts. This is why Crowley called the 2 the beginning—instead of the Ace—because now it is recognizable. The Ace was the origination, the point, and the 2 is the creation of the origination, the line. It is a going forward with the harmony of two poles working together.

3
A Formation. Nurturing.
Understanding. Planning. Developing. Uncertainty or certainty. Decision or indecision. Incompleteness. Striving. Yourself and other people. Taking care of energy.

The 3 is executing and evolving. It is striving after what the 1 conceived and the 2 created. It is doing, arriving, becoming, but it is not yet the completion of the 4. A 3 may indicate group activity with people, or it may involve yourself and something you are doing with other things. Nearly always there is some sort of decision to be made, some step to be taken, or some conclusion to be drawn. If it is experienced positively you will arrive at a decision or be certain of your action. If it is experienced negatively, you will feel uncertain and indecisive, unable to arrive at any definite conclusion to allow you to go on to the 4. If, at the 3, you cannot go on to the 4, you will start over again at 1 and begin the process over again, usually in some similar form.

4
An Expression. Manifesting.
Solidification. Materialization. Structure and building.
Security. Foundation. Stability. Protection. Clinging.
Being possessive. Brings order, sometimes with a sense of
limitation. Authority. Peace. Completeness. Ordering up
energy.

The 1, 2, and 3 have become reality in the 4. Something is being
done, after the formation of the 3. If positive, you feel peace and
success, a sense of completeness and accomplishment. The negative part of 4 may not want to move on to the 5. Now that
stability has been achieved after so much hard work, you may
be reluctant to let go of it. The 4 can mean clinging to or being
protective of something much loved or needed; possessing something for yourself and wanting to keep it; protecting your way of
life or whatever it is you want to keep secure. This is not seen as
bad negative (as negative simply refers to the opposite of
positive—creating a balance). It is often natural and good to rest
a while at 4, to enjoy the fruits of your labor, to rest your feet for
awhile. It may be that you are content where you are at 4 and
have no desire to carry that particular ambition further at this
point. There is beauty in allowing and enjoying accomplishment
and goals without wanting more. The 4 can be very protective,
and often you are protecting something of value and worth.
However, the negative can also be seen in cases where you
stagnate or become too possessive, and then you not only lose
your sense of balance, but you may be unable to change or move
forward.

5
A Movement. Continuing on.
Motion. Adjustment. Restlessness. Energy. Change.
Action.

It is time for change. The time has passed during the 4 when reward was reaped, but now it's time to move on. The contraction, or coming together, of 1 through 3 was experienced at 4. After it has been gotten together, it must be scattered; what has been contracted must be expanded. This usually comes in the form of change, action, adjustment or activity, all words implying scattering and expansion. Sometimes you willingly make this choice for yourself, but if not, the change is made for you. Sometimes the adjustment is good and is felt to be long overdue, so that it is a time of eagerly anticipated modification. But sometimes the 5 involves turmoil of some kind because gain also implies loss of the comfort of the 4. The 5 can also be undergoing a flurry of activity, being busy and on the go, a time of extreme activity from suddenly finding that you have too many irons in the fire. Or it is mental or emotional restlessness running around in the mind, such as worry or anxiety.

6
A Cycle. Flowing.
Elements at their practical best. Harmonized and balanced. Order, beauty, balance. Harmony. Energy exchange. The natural flow of psychic energy. Giving and receiving exactly what one gives and receives. Enjoying the flow.

This is the natural next step after the first 5 steps. The expanded energy in the 5 is now flowing. Six for most people is positive because it signifies near-perfect balance and order of whatever we had to get together in the 5.

7
A Rest. Waiting.
Hidden. Hesitation. Pausing. Unbalanced. Inability to go forward. Inner work. A time of evaluation, essentially an inner process of some kind. Indefinite and internal. Group animal intuition.

The number 7 cannot be better explained than in two verses from Genesis in the Bible describing the seventh day: "And on the seventh day, God ended his work which he had made, and he rested on the seventh day from all his work which he had made. And God blessed the seventh day and sanctified it: because that in it he had rested from all his work which God created and made."[1]

In a nation where 75 percent of its people are extraverts, this resting business is often a difficult thing to do! Americans are not at their best when being indefinite and internal. It is, however, a most necessary step in the process, and a wholly valuable one. Whereas it may seem a time of imbalance, it is really the step in which balance is obtained out of imbalance. Viewed positively, as a Cup might view it, it is the pause that refreshes. We have time to re-evaluate and re-access ourselves or our position. Viewed negatively, as a Disc might, it can indicate restlessness, boredom, worry, or fear. As with the other numbers, if the 7 is undertaken on our own volition, it is enjoyable. If, however,

---

[1]Biblical references in this text are from the Holy Bible, King James Version (Cleveland: The World Publishing Company). Here I refer to Genesis, chapter 2:2,3.

it is forced on us, it may be experienced as fear or inability to face self or an issue.

8
A Resolution. Going forward.
Reaction. Use of energy. Power. Will. Strength. Entering some new phase. Definite and external. Opening the door. Individual pure reason.

In the 7, you were unable to open the door. You stood behind the closed door, unsure of what might be on the other side. Finally, after what may seem an indeterminably long time, you work through the 7, and begin the 8. You go forward with newly-found strength and open the door. From the internal 7 you gain courage and power, and arrive at a resolution. You are willing to brave the risk because you realize you want to, you should, or that you have no choice. Either way, you now have a direction.

9
A Culmination. Completing.
Change with stability. The fullest development of the force in its relation to the forces above it. Contains combined energy of all preceding cards. The answer to the question. The height of a cycle. Finality. Culmination.

This is the peak of the cycle. The goal has been reached. Usually you are aware of this, but sometimes in the 9, as in the 1, the unconscious has not yet notified the conscious. If this is the case, and you are not yet fully cognizant of the completion, you soon will be when you reach 10. But for now, you can at least see the light at the end of the tunnel. The end of this cycle has, in fact, been reached.

10
A Fullness. Fulfilling.
End of all energy. Success. The beginning of a new cycle on a higher level. Transformation. An overview of the element. An overabundance of the element of the suit. A transition to something new, a transforming event. The whole of the matter as we know it—contains all the numbers. Being full of the element.

This is being *full* of the element. The first 9 processes have been experienced, and now you have moved over into the 10. Positively, it is being full of joy and happiness, a spiritually or materially rewarding time when you feel you are on top of the world and nothing could possibly be more perfect. Negatively, it is being full of depression, anger, or sorrow, a depleting time when you feel you have reached the end of your rope. Your back is up against the wall, and in defeat, you give up. This is why the 10 is also a beginning because it is only when we let go of energy that it is free to move. The 10 is an Ace plus the 9 preceding cards, so it signifies both beginnings and endings.

DIVINING WITH THE NUMBERS

When attempting to figure out the meaning of a certain number or card in a reading, the other cards in the layout give all-important clues. All the cards in a layout together tell the story, and all cards must be incorporated to get the full meaning. It is human nature to latch on to the most negative number or card in the reading because of our natural aversion to something bad possibly happening. None of us wants a bad answer, and that negative card or two lying there staring us right in the face is sometimes difficult to shake. But it is *all* the cards in the reading that make for the total story, so look to the desirable cards as well, the ones that may mitigate the disquieting one, or explain how it will all go together quite well in the end.

The numbers are an all-important aspect of the tarot. They are so integral that divination can be done with numbers alone, as in numerology. Numbers tell a story all their own, and when we combine them with the other components of tarot they tell us a complete story. By learning the essential principle of the number it can then be applied to the other ingredients of suit, color, cards and symbols that are shown in a card layout so we can obtain a collective answer by using the sum of its parts.

For example, let's combine the number 4 with each suit so we can see what happens when only the two components of suit and number are added together. In each case we will apply the number 4 to some area that is dominant to each suit. The 4 of Wands can mean we are clinging to independence, the 4 of Cups—clinging to dreams, 4 of Swords—clinging to control, the 4 of Discs—clinging to security.

If we apply the number 6 to all the suits, we might say that the 6 of Wands is flowing with one's intuition and higher self, the 6 of Cups is flowing with one's feelings and understanding of surrounding conditions, the 6 of Swords is flowing with a mental overview combined with great mental stability, and the 6 of Discs is flowing with steadiness and realization. Again, all we have done is apply the essence of the number to the essence of the suit. These examples are just a few possibilities out of many, and it is all the cards together in a reading which enable us to pick the possibility that is likely to manifest.

Since all archetypes contain within themselves both the yin and yang of their whole nature, we may well ask how we are to know if a number or card is going to be experienced positively or negatively. How can the person who is seriously interested in learning about the cards and himself or herself hope to sort out not only all the different meanings of the cards, but also the dark and the light of each of those meanings?

Any experienced reader can tell you that it's not easy! It takes study, hard work, constant practice, and most of all, *desire*. Reading the tarot is not an art that can be learned in just a few years or less. It takes intensive study, hard work, and dedication to become a decent doctor or attorney, and it also takes time and study to be able to read the cards. There are no quick roads or shortcuts. In truth, it is a lifetime study, one in which no matter how far we progress, we will always be a student.

Like any skill we set out to master, all parts of the learning process must be undergone, and when we have learned them, we move onto another level where we learn them all over again, and then again and again at each successive level. Not only is this an intellectual process, it is also an emotional, spiritual, and physical process that must be studied, lived, understood and fully integrated into the individual. Intuition alone is not enough, and neither is knowledge, nor experience, nor feelings. All four must become embodied within us.

CHAPTER 8

The Four Suits

In a deck of playing cards there are four suits—clubs, hearts, spades and diamonds. In a tarot deck these same four suits are called wands, cups, swords and discs respectively. In both decks each of the four suits is numbered 1 through 10, making a total of forty pip cards in each deck. In some tarot decks the four suits are also shown with pips, just as in playing decks, but in others the minor cards have been illustrated with pictures or symbols. Regardless of how they are illustrated, the four suits of a playing deck are the same as the Minor Arcana of the tarot, consisting of 10 wands (clubs), 10 cups (hearts), 10 swords (spades), and 10 discs (diamonds).

The four suits are another way of describing the four elements. These four elements possess certain properties—each element being individually endowed with its own inherent code pattern—and becoming familiar with these inherent codes is how we are able to attribute certain characteristics to the four suits.

In the esoteric, or hidden, sciences we find nearly all work based upon the belief that everything in our solar system is composed of these four elements. Virtually everything can be broken down into one or more of these four elements because everything is composed of them in one way or another. In metaphysical terminology these four elements are known as fire, water, air, and earth. The ancient science of alchemy is the study of these four elements, and the alchemists referred to them as sulphur, mercury, azoth, and salt. Humanistic psychologists call them intuition, feeling, thinking, and sensation, respectively. But no matter what they are called, they still remain the same four elements from which we derive the four suits—wands (fire), cups (water), swords (air), and discs (earth).

The human body is composed of fire, water, air and earth. Fire radiates through the body as thermal heat. Some time ago a type of radiant photography (called Kirlian photography) revealed this thermal heat as it luminated from the body to form a thermal spectrum diffusing outward from it. Physicians call it body heat—metaphysicians call it the aura. Scientists tell us that over 85 percent of our body is composed of water. Air is located between each and every cell in our body, in our organs, in our blood and skin, and we breathe this air into the body through our lungs, constantly replenishing our need for it. The earth part of our body is the obvious part—teeth, nails, bones, organs, muscles, skin, etc. The physical body consists mostly of carbon, oxygen, and hydrogen, all found in abundance in the earth.

Fire, water, air, and earth are not found in just specific parts of the body but are interspersed throughout every single cell. So it is with the four processes of archetypes in everything. In order to better study the parts of any whole, we break it down into parts, but in real life there really is no clear-cut demarcation where one begins and the other ends. Bones are not only earth, just as perspiration is not only water. Although bones and perspiration have materialized a main portion of a certain element, they still contain within themselves all four elements. But because archetypes do partake of their own likenesses, because like-attracts-like, which is why bones materialize mostly earth and perspiration mostly water, we are able to look at forms and deduce their most characteristic element. This is how we are able to make correspondences, how we can say which part of an archetype will be dominant in its expression. Table 1 on pages 75–77 lists some corresponding quadruplicities of the four elements, or suits.

Table 1. Quadruplicities of the Four Suits.

WANDS	CUPS	SWORDS	DISCS
Clubs	Hearts	Spades	Diamonds
Fire	Water	Air	Earth
Intuition	Feeling	Thinking	Sensation[a]
Spirit body	Emotional body	Mental body	Earth body
The spiritual world of creativity	The emotional world of feeling	The mental world of pure ideas	The material world of visible objects
Consciousness-raising	Heart opening	Mind expansion	Body sustaining[b]
Unseen self-organizing	Absorption and assimilation	Expansion and celebration	Memory and remembering
Instinct and intuition	Emotions and imagination	Intellect and illusion	Establishment and endurance rule[c]
EVOKES the Force	CHANNELS the Force	CHANGES the Force	GROUNDS the Force
Kings	Queens	Princes	Princesses
Ace of Wands	Ace of Cups	Ace of Swords	Ace of Discs
0 Aries	0 Cancer	0 Libra	0 Capricorn
March 21	June 21	September 23	December 21
Spring equinox	Summer solstice	Fall equinox	Winter solstice
Spring	Summer	Fall	Winter
South	East	West	North
Masculine-Yang	Feminine-Yin	Masculine-Yang	Feminine-Yin

Table 1. Quadruplicities of the Four Suits (continued).

WANDS	CUPS	SWORDS	DISCS
Aries, Leo, Sagittarius	Cancer, Scorpio, Pisces	Gemini, Libra, Aquarius	Taurus, Virgo, Capricorn
Salamanders	Undines	Sylphs	Gnomes
Power	Love	Death	Wealth
Creativity	Psychism	Struggle	Money
Career	Dreams	Ideas	Work
Self	Fantasy	Ego	Security
Passion	Pleasure	Commitment	Effort
Conceives	Nurtures	Utilizes	Materializes
Masters	Serves	Changes	Produces
Happiness	Flowing	Fighting	Melancholy
Courage	Patience	Extremes	Determination
I want	I feel	I think	I do
Strength	Passivity	Energy	Persistence
Lion	Eagle	Man	Bull
He	Vah	Yod	He
Red (fire tones)	Blue (water tones)	Sky blue and lavendar (sky tones)	Greens and browns (earth tones)
Moves in straight lines	Balanced movement	Moves by whirling and vortexes	Arresting movement
Seeing	Tasting	Touching	Smelling
Kinetic	Space	Time	Inertia[d]
To desire	To know	To dare	To keep silent[e]

Table 1. Quadruplicities of the Four Suits (continued).

WANDS	CUPS	SWORDS	DISCS
Radiant	Fluid	Gaseous	Solid[f]
Sulphur	Mercury	Azoth	Salt[g]
Depth of prayer or any form of concentration	Subtlety of feelings and understanding of surrounding conditions	Development of full consciousness	Steadiness in realization[h]
Power of command	Dionysiac ecstasy, the source of divine inspiration	Discernment which banishes error	The support which magic symbols offer to the learned[i]
Transformation	Insight	Concentration	Purification[j]
Origination	Creation	Formation	Expression[k]

[a]Jungian Functions
[b]Mary Greer uses these four terms (read horizontally) in her book *Tarot for Yourself* (N. Hollywood, CA: Newcastle Publishing Co., Inc., 1984) to describe the aces of the four suits (pp. 219–220). They are key concepts from Tarot teacher and counselor Suzanne Judith.
[c]Mode
[d]Metaphysical
[e]Astral
[f]Physical
[g]Alchemical
[h]Hermetism
[i]Magic
[j]Meditation
[k]Qaballistic

From this list of corresponding quadruplicities we see that certain words and forms are synonymous in their meanings. If their parallels are memorized and applied, they can be an invaluable aid in comprehending the structure of the tarot. They help bring together what at first appears to be a mish-mash of non-related ideas into a concise and interchangeable whole.

Each phrase under *Wands* applies to the suit of wands, and all wand cards share these characteristics. The same applies to the other three suits. The first four correspondences need to be memorized when you study tarot. See Table 2.

Table 2. Basic Suit Interrelationships.

Tarot Suit	Playing Card Suit	Element	Psychological Function
Wands	Clubs	Fire	Intuition
Cups	Hearts	Water	Feeling
Swords	Spades	Air	Thinking
Discs	Diamonds	Earth	Sensation

It doesn't really matter where you start on this list or what you prefer to call the four elements. They are all different names for the same four inherent code-principles. There is no one starting point or dominant leader. The four correlations in Table 2 are the names we use to tie the four elements to the cards, but the four elements are actually four groupings, or processes, which are found in all life. Quoting from J.C. Cirlot's invaluable book, *A Dictionary of Symbols*:

> Basically, all these problems of 'origin' are of very secondary importance. From the point of view of symbolist tradition, there is no question of priority, only of simultaneity: all phenomena are parallel and related. Interpretations only indicate the starting-point of the interpreter, not the causal or prior condition within the system itself.

> The apparent multiplicity of outward forms spreading out over concentric planes is deceptive, for, in the last resort, all the phenomena of the universe can be

reduced to a few basic rhythmic forms, grouped and ordered by the passage of time.[1]

The following list shows a few of these basic rhythmic forms, grouped and ordered by suit.

———————————— WANDS ————————————

Element: Fire

Archetypal pattern: The archetypal world of unseen organizing. The spiritual world of creativity (spirit body). This is the power of the Self to organize the self in unseen activity before bringing it to actuality. Symmetries formed in the unconscious and conscious. The organized action of bringing the parts into a whole.

Mode: Instinct and intuition. Wands perceive and function through the modes of instinct and intuition. The definition of intuition is "to look to see inside." Instinct is Latin for "impulse." A wand uses both or either of these two modes in life situations and in perceiving personal reality.

Action: Evokes the force.

Astrological phrases: I am; I will; I perceive.

Key word: Consciousness-raising.

Wands represent creativity, enterprise, career. They have great energy, power, inspiration and aspiration, drive, desire, and passion. Freedom is the breath of life to them. They can display direct honesty, great faith, enthusiasm, unending strength, love, happiness, pleasure, joy, high spirits, and independence. They can also be self-involved, headstrong, consumed with a passion to the exclusion of everything else, and possess false pride.

---

[1]J.E. Chirlot, *A Dictionary of Symbols* (New York: Philosophical Library, 1971), pp. xxxiii, xliv.

Events for wands involve energies that are harmonically resonant with the wand's archetypal blueprint. Events manifest as situations revolving around inner-self, power, creativity, career, and all dynamics of the spiritual world of creativity. Any of the wand key words and descriptions apply to the nature of the wand event. All events **evoke**. Because wands are spirit and unseen organizing, the physical events are like the season of Spring—evoking, coming forth, inspirational, exciting, passionate, arising, powerful, free, issuing, and originating.

CUPS

Element: Water

Archetypal pattern: The archetypal world of absorption and assimilation. The emotional world of feeling (emotional body). This is the power of the Self to absorb, assimilate and dissolve the self. The ability to bring in sensitivity and stimulus from the world and to assimilate it into oneself for absorption and dissolution.

Mode: Emotions and imagination. Cups react to life through their emotions and imagination. They experience life through their feeling function. If they cannot feel it they can imagine it. They have the greatest capacity for imagination, which is why many are psychics, poets, artists, and musicians.

Action: Channels the force.

Astrological phrases: I feel; I need; I believe.

Key words: Heart opening.

Cups represent relationships, the psychic realm, fantasy, pleasure, serenity, introversion, and nurturing. Cups can display sensitivity, emotional yearning, vitality, patience, sympathy, compassion, forbearance, tolerance, and appreciation. Cups can also be oversensitive, confused, easily influenced; may daydream to excess; incline toward addiction and laziness; they may inadvertently create crises and cultivate upheavals.

Events for cups are any of those occurrences containing rhythms that are harmonically oscillatory with the cup's archetypal blueprint. Events manifest as situations concerning relationships, love, psychism, and all dynamics of the emotional world of feeling. All key words pertaining to cups apply to the nature of cup events. The main word describing all cup events is **channeling**, because the situation will always be one similar to Summer—channeling, absorbing, emoting, flowing, deepening, nurturing, warm, supportive, bearing, substantial, and basking.

SWORDS

Element: Air

Archetypal pattern: The archetypal world of expansion and celebration. The mental world of pure ideas (mental body). This is the power of the Self to change and expand the self. Whatever is absorbed and assimilated long enough becomes superconcentrated and demands to be given form and released.

Mode: Intellect and illusion. Swords experience their realities through their mind and thought processes. Their two modes of perceiving are intellect and illusion. If it doesn't fit into their personal intellectual frame-of-reference, they make it fit.

Action: Changes the force.

Astrological phrases: I think; I weigh; I know.

Key words: Mind expansion.

Swords represent the intellect, mind, ego, the conscious, volatility, crises, ideas, teaching and preaching, striving, rational thought, and extremes. Of all the suits they have the greatest need to be around people. Swords can display penetration, sociability, excellent senses, changeability, eccentricity, rational thinking, and detachment. Swords can also be deceitful, narrow-minded, judgemental, controlling, possessive, jealous, inconsistent, and defensive. They can relish struggle, problems, gossip, and conflicts.

Events for swords are all those situations containing code patterns that spirally lattice with the sword's archetypal blueprint. Events that manifest in physical happenings include expansion, scattering, news, crises, and all grounding of the mental world of pure ideas. Any of the swords' key phrases and descriptions apply to the actions of the sword event. Swords and their events are like the season of Fall, which, like Spring for wands, is a very apropos name. The nature of swords is **change**, and as does Fall, they change, expunge, break up, disorganize, undo, dispel, shake, delete, are volatile, extreme, blustery, blow hard, and scatter to the winds. But what is often forgotten about swords is that Fall is also a time of maturity, a time of peak expansion, so that change can also be experienced as a beautiful, awe-inspiring time where all the beautiful colors we've ever dared to dream of are celebrated.

DISCS

Element: Earth

Archetypal pattern: The archetypal world of memory and remembering. The material world of visible physical objects (earth body). Without the power to remember, the symmetry is not completed. Knowledge is memory, and unless we remember "to know" we cannot make it visible. This is the power of the Self to know self and to become aware of Self by memory. Knowledge is remembered in physical objects.

Mode: Establishment and endurance. A disc perceives the world through the five physical senses. Discs perceive *only* what they can see, hear, touch, taste, and smell. They see what is established and enduring and react with endurance and stamina or by long-established ingrained automatic habits.

Action: Grounds the force.

Astrological phrases: I have; I serve; I use.

Key words: Body sustaining.

Discs represent work, money, security, finances, earthly rewards for effort, business and material success, possessions, material needs, traditions, foundations, and solidity. Discs can display a large appetite, attachments, dependability, stability, knowledge, skills, practicality, being cautious, careful, thorough, and exact. Discs can also be inflexible, petrifying, greedy, overly attached, anxious, overbearing, and may suffer from the inability to abstract or change.

Events for discs are all those events incurring energies that are harmonically resonant with the discs' archetypal blueprint. Events manifest as situations revolving around work, money, possessions, traditions, and all dynamics of the material world of visible physical objects. Any of the discs' key words, modes, and descriptions apply to the nature of the disc event. The key action for disc events is **grounding**. A disc event is always like the season of Winter—grounding, crystallizing, arresting, materializing, viable, firm, definite, tangible, solid, thorough, physical, and as compared to the other three suits, inert, because it is energy in its most crystalline form.

DIVINING WITH THE SUITS

When reading characteristics attributable to the suits, numbers, and individual cards, there are numerous qualities to bring together in order to make a meaningful synopsis out of the reading. In order to be as accurate as possible, a couple of concepts should be kept in mind:

1) *The archetypes exist and interact on all levels.* Archetypes are multi-dimensional and oscillate in patterns that interconnect and weave in and out of our realities with a complexity of networks beyond our grasp. Each card and each layout not only contains within itself the polarity of its own seeming opposition but also the many different aspects and forms of its archetypal gridwork. The best we can do is hope to obtain their partial meanings as they relate to our lives through the synchronicity of the cards. These descriptions of the suits, and any description of anything, depend not only upon the reality of the situation and people involved but also upon the level(s) in which the archetypes are operating. And we cannot really ever know just how or at exactly what level an archetype will express. But because like-attracts-like according to archetypal principle, and because the archetype is active at all levels, we can make educated guesstimates at how it will display its code-principle if we adjust our purpose and design to concur with its resonance.

For example, in the list of quadruplicities I have said that wands represent south, cups east, swords west, and discs north. Wands are south because the south is hot and arid, like fire. We know that birds fly south for the winter because they go where it's hot. Cups are east because the east is cool, revitalizing, and refreshing, like water. The breeze and light as the sun rises in the east every morning is both refreshing and revitalizing, which is why plants are happy facing east. Swords are west, for the west is glaring, expiring and extreme, like air. Plants are unhappy facing west because the sun is too intense and dry. Lastly, discs are north because the north is cold, ossifying and frozen, like earth. Naturalists know that moss grows on the north side of a tree because the north side of a tree is the coolest. Wind blowing from the south is hot, from the east cool, from the west stifling, and wind blowing from the north is cold.

Most of us will agree with this interpretation because from our point of view where we live in the western hemisphere this is true. It is not true, however, for those people, creatures, and trees living in other hemispheres. For them, south, east, west, and north are just the opposite, all turned around. Our north wind is their south wind, our west wind their east. That is because our angles are different. Same planet, same wind, same direction, but different angles.

Similarly, the four directions take on a different meaning if we suggest a different purpose other than physical for them. For the purposes of magic, wands are not south, but north, and discs are not north, but south, because from an esoteric view the physical (discs and north) is seen as a mirror reflection of the spiritual (wands and south). In magic, two of the directions mirror reflections to the physical plane, while two do not, thus when taken as a complete unity of four, they represent both the inner and outer in a harmonious unity.

Likewise, we run into other seeming contradictions when running from left to right on the quadruplicity chart, so that many times we find people who believe Kings are not fire, but earth, and Princesses are not earth, but fire. In meditation some people see transformation as earth and purification as spirit, instead of vice versa. One reason the quadruplicities are perceived differently is because their interpretation depends on whether a person is striving toward the spirit world or the physical world. Transformation to one means transformation of spirit, to another it means transformation of physical. Of course, in reality there is no difference, and just like the human cell, all four elements are in one package, and no one is going anywhere. But because we can only see any one indivisible whole by its parts, or by our angle on the subject, we see a difference, which is what creates all the confusion to begin with. When explaining anything using time and space, as we must here on the physical level, we are forced to speak in terms of direction, levels, planes, where in actuality, there are no such things.

Crowley does an excellent job of explaining this concept in *The Book of Thoth* when he describes why the court cards are often confused. The Princess grows up, marries a Prince, and becomes the Queen. The Prince grows up, marries a Princess, and becomes the King. And if things weren't bad enough, in royalty the King often married his own daughter, which makes her both the Queen and a Princess at the same time.

The point is, all things are not only according to each person's reality and angle, but also include such infinite complexities that to state a permanent "definite" in most cases is simply to display our own ignorance. Everything in the universe can be thought of in this way. This does not negate the very real characteristics of singularly arranged energies—it only brings into consideration the fact that just as the human body is composed of all four elements that cannot be considered apart from themselves, neither can any suit nor archetype, and interpretation depends not only on viewpoint but also on application.

2) *The second concept to keep in mind when reading the cards is projections.* Again, this is angle, and even though we all project, it is hopefully our job as a card reader to try to keep our own projections to a minimum. What we do not recognize within ourselves as belonging to ourselves, we project onto the outer world and onto others to play out for us, for it is not what our conscious thinks that creates our reality, but what our subconscious believes.

Commonly, cup people will project that other people perceive as they do, more or less, and disc people will project that other people perceive as they do, give or take numerous differences, and so on through the suits, when nothing could be further from the truth. Because we fail to comprehend that others are not like us, we believe that we can give the same advice to others that we would give to ourselves. To *know* that each person is a complete and totally unique individual that thinks and sees *alone* is a grace. People are motivated not a little differently, but a lot differently. We all know our worlds differently, experience all things differently.

For instance, I have attributed the quality of mastering to wands. Sword people may read this and exclaim, "That's not right. Wands don't master, Swords do!" And from a sword viewpoint, this is true. Indeed, it is common for all the suits to see swords as very much into mastering because swords can be far more motivated than any other suit to control their environment and influence others. But in wand context, the true essence of mastering is the mastering of self, not others. Wand people are interested in mastering themselves, or whatever interests them whereas sword people are interested in mastering others. So wand people master in a wand's way, for self, and sword people master in a sword's way, for ego-conscious or group-conscious. Indeed, cup people attempt to master emotions, and disc people their physical security. Although each suit masters, it has been listed as an attribute of wands because, wholistically speaking, we must first master ourselves before we can truly master anything else.

Each suit reads and understands from its own viewpoint. Any word, whether it be mastering, working, playing, loving, boredom, or freedom, means something totally different to every person. It is projection when we try to apply a sword meaning to a wand context. Boredom to some is being alone, boredom to others is being with people. Loving to some is giving, loving to others is receiving.

In these descriptions I have attempted to put each suit in its own context as seen through its own eyes. Admittedly, this is quite an impossibility to say the very least, so I can only ask for the reader's tolerance and patience. All things are seen through the eyes of the beholder's own personal reality, and when interrupting the cards, all we can attempt to do is not see ourselves in the other fellow, not to believe that he is like us, to the best of our ability.

CHAPTER 9

The Court Cards

*T*here are four court cards for each of the four suits, making a total of sixteen court cards in a tarot deck. These are the King, Queen, Prince, and Princess of each suit. In a deck of playing cards there are three court cards for each of the four suits, making a total of twelve court cards. These are the King, Queen and Jack of each suit.

How four court cards came to be three court cards, or vice versa, is another one of those debates that will most likely never be resolved, but there are several theories. Some authorities think it's likely that originally the first decks had four court cards and somewhere along their historical path four court cards evolved into only three, this being done by combining what was the Page and Knight in the tarot into what has become the one single Jack in today's playing cards. This is certainly a logical conclusion, except for the fact that in some of the very earliest decks it is the Queen who is missing, so it may be it was the Queen who was later added.

We would be amiss if we didn't mention the synchronicity of three court cards for playing cards and four for tarot. It's widely known that most religious concepts are based on a cycle of three, or a trinity. The trinity figures prominently in Christianity, regardless of denomination, and in other religions as well. It is usually in the mystical branches of popular religions (Qabalistic, Sufi, Hermetic or Gnostic) that we find the idea of three powers replaced by the idea of four. It probably isn't any coincidence that there are three court cards for the masses and four for the mystics.

The King, Queen, Prince and Princess have different titles depending on the creator of the deck. Some of these are:

King–Emperor, Knight, Priest, Chief, Man, Father
Queen–Empress, Priestess, Matriarch, Woman, Mother
Prince–Knight, Son, Warrior, Brother
Princess–Page, Daughter, Maiden, Child, Squire, Sister

Many writers begin their discussion of court cards by pointing out that court cards present the greatest confusion and diversity of all the cards, and, boy, is this true!

Some scholars of the tarot claim that court cards are people; some claim they are events; still others claim the court cards are both people and events. Some say that the court cards represent yourself, and some say they represent other people. And then, of course, some authorities say they represent both! Anyone who has attempted to figure this out can tell you that it's no easy task doing a reading when a court card can represent an event, a situation, a person, yourself or someone else, someone else involved in a situation, or yourself involved with someone else, or perhaps, an event that you find yourself involved in with someone else concerning a situation. It's no wonder that some of us throw our hands up in exasperation and secretly wish that the court cards would do a disappearing act! Actually, what many people end up doing is just sort of glossing over any court card received in a reading.

There are several reasons for all this confusion. But first of all, before we go on, it is only right to make clear just exactly what it is the court cards indeed are. *The court cards are people.* They are *not* events. They are *not* situations. They are *only* people.

Now, having made that perfectly clear, let me add what may at first appear to muddy up the waters a bit again. The reason court cards are often confused with events is because people are like the events that happen to them. People are the main actors in the events and situations that occur in their lives, and because like-attracts-like, the symmetries of certain people will always involve them in the symmetries of events similar to the personality. A devoted wife and mother isn't likely to be found in the neighborhood bar, and a construction worker isn't likely to be found crocheting doilies. This does not mean the court cards should be interpreted as events or situations, but as characters involved in a situation of their likeness.

COURT CARDS AS SIGNIFICATORS

Since the beginning of our knowledge of court cards, we have known about their use as significators. The significator is the card chosen to represent the person being read for. If we could go back far enough, we would probably find that originally court cards were *only* used to represent people.

When doing a reading, most of us are likely to want to stick with the interpretation of court cards that we first learned, and if this is proving satisfactory for you, then by all means, continue. However, if you find that court cards are confusing, you might want to use the following method to employ them as the significator only. This is not instruction on how to do a full reading, which is discussed later in chapter 13, but is only about how to employ the court cards as people.

Separate the court cards from the rest of the deck. Choose your significator, place it in front of you at what will be the center of your layout. Put all the other court cards aside. The only time the court cards should be involved in this first laying out of the cards is for the significator. Then shuffle and lay out the Major and Minor Arcana to do your reading. This method will give you precise accuracy that does not end up giving you three or four people for a question where you need the specific details of the Minor and will answer your question clearly and concisely. After you have laid out the cards, if you have a desire to know more about the people involved in the issue, you can take the court cards, shuffle them separately from the rest of the deck, and place them in the house or layout where you wish to know more about a certain person who may be involved. Court cards are wonderful tools for describing any particular person you may be interested in when laid upon the house in question.

It is natural to want to use the entire deck all at once when doing a reading because this seemingly simplifies matters and because nearly all books do it this way, but in the end, it does not simplify matters at all, and it is frustrating to ask for the outcome of a situation and receive a court card for an answer. This not only does not answer the question, it often poses another because a court card is not an event nor is it a situation—it is a person and should be treated as such.

COURT CARDS AS PSYCHOLOGICAL TYPES

The court cards show the sixteen different personalities of people frequently recognized as psychological types. Psychology breaks these sixteen personality types into three categories: (1) by their approach to life—introvert or extravert; (2) by their main function—intuition, feeling, thinking, or sensation; (3) and by their attitude—judging or perceptive. In order to understand the court cards, we must first attempt to understand people, and psychology is a tool we can employ to do this. The Golden Dawn teachings apparently worked with this method before psychologists, but modern psychology has now categorized the method into a testing tool that can determine a person's personality type.

To study sixteen psychological types in any depth is a task that requires its own book, and once again, Carl Jung has helped us with this. In his categorization of personalities, Jung divided people into two groups—extraverts and introverts. These two groups were further broken down into four functions, which he called intuitive (fire), feeling (water), thinking (air), and sensation (earth). As you can immediately see, these are the four suits. Jung originally made eight divisions, each division describing the various combinations possible with four of the functions being introverted and four of the functions being extraverted.[1] Later, Briggs and Myers added attitudes — judging and perceptive as a third category.[2]

Jung's material on the psychology of types is profound and highly recommended to anyone interested in learning more about the court cards. First we will discuss the three major categories, then later the sixteen individual personality types.

Extraverts and Introverts

Starting with the first major division, everyone is either an extravert or an introvert. Some of their comparable characteristics (as based upon the MBTI) are shown in Table 3 on page 94.

Because extraverts make up the majority of the population, because most men are extraverts, and because extraverts are the doers, the sociable, the physical and people-oriented, nearly all of Western society is based on extraversion. Introverts are highly protective of their main function—they do not normally use it when dealing with the outside world. This means that introverts are typically at a disadvantage in society. Introverts receive stimulus from within, and thus reserve true expression for the inner world. People can know introverts without ever really knowing them, although usually only the introvert knows this!

Whereas introverts are usually out of their element in groups, they can literally shine on a one-to-one basis, and as

---

[1]C.G. Jung, *Psychological Types* (Princeton, NJ: Princeton University Press, 1971).

[2]To avoid confusion on the part of the reader, the author would like to note that Katherine Briggs and her daughter, Isabel Briggs Myers, developed the Myers-Briggs Type Indicator (MBTI) referred to in this book. However, it was Isabel Briggs Myers, along with her son Peter Myers, who wrote *Gifts Differing* (Palo Alto, CA: Consulting Psychologists Press, 1980), which discusses the MBTI and on which were based the types and characteristics tables included in this chapter.

Table 3. Trait of Extraverts and Introverts.

Extravert	Introvert
The afterthinkers; cannot understand life until they have lived it.	The forethinkers; cannot live life until they understand it.
Minds are outwardly directed, interest and attention following objective happenings, primarily those of the immediate environment.	Minds are inwardly directed, frequently unaware of the objective environment, interest and attention being engrossed by inner events.
Understandable and accessible, often sociable, more at home in the world of people and things than in the world of ideas.	Subtle and impenetrable, often taciturn and shy, more at home in the world of ideas than in the world of people and things.
Typical weakness lies in a tendency toward intellectual superficiality, very conspicuous in extreme types.	Typical weakness lies in a tendency toward impracticality, very conspicuous in extreme types.*
When depressed, wants to be around people.	When depressed, wants to be alone.
Receives energy from people.	Energy drained by people.

*The comparisons above are taken from *Gifts Differing* by Isabel Briggs Myers with Peter Myers. (Palo Alto, CA: Consulting Psychologists Press, 1980), p. 56.

opposed to the extraverts who may have many, but perhaps less deep friendships, introverts may have few, but very deep, relationships. It is extremely difficult to be an introvert in our society, especially for men, for introversion is not rewarded nor particularly respected. It is considered cool to be macho, physical, sports-oriented, and socially adept; it is nerdy to be quiet, intellectual, and withdrawn.

The Four Functions

In addition to everyone either being an extravert or an introvert, everyone also is one of four basic personality types, which are called the four functions, as we discussed when describing the four suits. Jung devoted a large portion of his life to the study of alchemy and some believe that from the four alchemical elements he may have derived these four basic psychological types. His book, *Psychological Types*, is based on his theory that all people perceive through one superior function, use one auxiliary function, seldom use the third function, and suppress the fourth, also called the inferior function. Jung believed that all human behavior, perception, and action is filtered through all people according to their own psychological arrangement of the four functions.

Each of us perceives all our world mainly through intuition, thinking, feeling, or sensation. We each have a superior function which motivates and drives us. It is our own personal set of rose-colored (or smoke-covered) glasses through which we see our world. We usually believe that others are perceiving and seeing the same way we are (more or less), and Jung called this erroneous assumption "projection." Most of us are not aware that we are projecting. We like to think that we do understand other people, but in fact, our perception of others is understood only by what we ourselves know and are. We may be able to intellectually grasp that someone is different and to verbally define someone's differences, even come to know what to expect from another person's behavior, but to actually see someone else's world as that other person does is a psychic function, not an intellectual one, and psychic functions must be personally lived and experienced to be known. They cannot be intellectualized because perceptions are internally experienced, in the realm of the psyche where all experiences are non-physical. The following four paragraphs give a brief summary and idea as to how each of the four functions perceives.

Intuitive people perceive the world through the sixth sense. They intuit the environment and base opinions and actions on their invisible "antennas." They usually can't tell someone why they are doing something in a certain way, only that somehow they "know." If intuitives are asked to describe a good book, they won't be able to go into detail, probably won't remember the author or the names of the main characters but will describe the book in terms of its overview. They will be able to relate to the theme of the book and its general message. There may be some arm and hand gesturing and a few exclamations and glittering generalities like, "It was wonderful!" in the attempt to relay the unseen impact the book had on them.

Feeling people perceive through emotions and feelings. They are motivated by what feels good or bad; how something makes them feel. For them, emotions determine the right or the wrong of a situation. When asked to describe a good book they've read, they usually respond with an emotional description, such as it was "so sad" or "so happy." A good book is a great escape from reality into another reality. They tend to personally identify with the characters, which is something that thinking and sensation people do *not* do. It is not unusual for feeling people to get so involved in a book or movie that for a while afterward they take on some of the traits of the character they have just been reading about.

Thinking people use their mind to filter the world. Everything is seen through the intellect. To be logical or to fit into an orderly pattern makes sense to them. Two and two equal four, and if they don't equal four, then it either doesn't exist or it has no merit. In relating to a good book, they can remember what chapter such-and-such was found in, and two months after reading the book can often quote certain passages almost verbatim. They typically may not read romances or fantasy, and these are seldom considered good books. Good books are those which reinforce their own personal mental conclusions.

Sensation people see the world through their five senses. If it can be seen, heard, smelled, touched, or tasted, it is real. They are extremely practical, and physical things are practical. Anything else may be considered impractical. They would describe a good book by its utilitarian function. They are also great at remembering vivid detail; for just as thinking people's minds are not clouded with feeling, sensation people's perceptions are not clouded with intuition. They tend toward physical renderings and detail rather than the overall meaning of the book.

These four functions are the basics. They are also the same descriptions of the four suits. Their attributes and detriments, and how these are combined within the individual, make up the individual's mode of perception.

All people also possess an auxiliary function, which is the function they use second-most. Whereas nearly all our perceptions are filtered through our superior function, we use our auxiliary function as a back-up system. Because our superior and auxiliary functions are our conscious way of perceiving, we are most comfortable with and know most about them. We are less comfortable with the inferior function, which we are not in touch with and which we have repressed into unconsciousness. Because we have repressed it, our inferior function is usually that part of us we deny or disown. And because we disown it, we tend to perceive its negative side in others.

It is important to note that our unconscious inferior function is *always* opposite our conscious superior function:

Superior	Inferior
Intuition	Sensation
Feeling	Thinking
Thinking	Feeling
Sensation	Intuition

So, if the main function is intuition, people will repress sensation. Since intuitive types repress sensation, they tend to not understand that type of behavior and tend to disrespect and misinterpret it in others. For instance, intuitive people will often see the sensation-dominant person as being picky, critical, stuffy, and boring instead of seeing sensation's finer attributes of stability, thoroughness, dependability, and loyalty.

Just because a function is repressed, however, does not mean it does not exist within the person—it very much does. Due to the inferior function being denied by the conscious, it fights to gain recognition and respect, and thus is that part of us that erupts in moments of anger, stress, or confusion. And this it normally does in its most negative form and with forceful impact, almost as if to pay us back for our earlier denial.

We can automatically know our inferior function if we know our superior, because they are always opposite. It is very important to know our superior and inferior functions because our superior is where we shine and possess natural talents, and our inferior is where we normally have trouble and problems—with ourselves and with other people. For example, thinking-dominant types, because they are not in touch with their emotions, typically have relationship problems. Sensation-dominant types often have problems being carefree and flexible because they don't know how to respond intuitively. Likewise, feeling types believe that thinking types are hard-hearted, calculating, and cold.

The study of personality functions is so fascinating and helpful to the average person that it is truly a tragedy it is not taught in our public schools. It could do so much to help people comprehend themselves and others, and attach less blame and more understanding to the differences of being human. It is a lengthy task however, and unfortunately, it is not possible to go into it in this book in the detail and explanation it deserves and needs. The superior and inferior functions are discussed a bit more in the chapter on the Minor Arcana.

Judging and Perceptive Attitudes

It was Carl Jung who initially conceived and wrote of psychological typology in its original form. But it was two women, Katharine C. Briggs, and her daughter, Isabel Briggs Myers, who took Jung's theory and expanded his original eight types into sixteen and added the attitudes of judging and perceptive. Working painstakingly for decades to evolve a pool that would accurately describe the attitudes, feelings, perceptions, and behaviors of the different psychological types, they eventually developed the MBTI (Myers-Briggs Type Indicator), which has become one of the most popular type-indicators used by humanistic psychologists and corporations today.

Their work and the MBTI is discussed in *Gifts Differing* written by Isabel Briggs Myers with her son Peter B. Myers. The differentiating characteristics of judging and perceptive types excerpted from their book are shown in Table 4 on page 100.

The interpretations used for the court cards in this book are largely based upon Myers-Briggs psychological types, plus some Golden Dawn descriptions which do not conflict with, but reinforce, the Jungian and Myers-Briggs theory. These descriptions indicate whether the individual is an introvert or an extravert, show the superior and auxiliary functions (thus also the inferior), and indicate whether the individual is a judging or perceptive type.

COURT CARDS AND THE ELEMENTS

It is more than a little interesting to note that most current court card meanings are derived from the Golden Dawn system and Aleister Crowley, who was once a member of the Golden Dawn, and that their descriptions coincide uncannily with Jung's and Myers-Briggs' theory of psychological types. There is some speculation that Jung might have had knowledge or contact with the

Table 4. Judging and Perceptive Types.*

Judging Type	Perceptive Type
Like to have matters settled and decided as promptly as possible, so that they will know what is going to happen and can plan for it and be prepared for it.	Like to keep decisions open as long as possible before doing anything irrevocable, because they don't know nearly enough about it yet.
Aim to be right.	Aim to miss nothing.
Take real pleasure in getting something finished, out of the way, and off their minds.	Take great pleasure in starting something new, until the newness wears off.
Inclined to regard the perceptive types as aimless drifters.	Inclined to regard the judging type as only half-alive.

*Briggs Myers and Myers, *Gifts Differing*, p. 75.

Golden Dawn, or at least with some of its members. On the other hand, maybe he didn't, and their arrival at similar conclusions is simply another example of one of Jung's famous synchronicities.

●　　●　　●

Princesses are learning their element. They are finishing what it is they have to finish by taking in energy—through learning, experience, and activity. This is why they are often seen as messengers. When a Princess is involved, we can expect those people either to bring or receive information.

Princes are utilizing their element. They are the next step past the Princess. After taking in the energy, they are putting it to work and working through it. They are focusing on the energy and expanding it.

In effect, both Princesses and Princes are learning their element. The Princess is doing it on the inner level, as an introvert, and the Prince is doing it as an extravert. For example, the Prince of Cups learns about physical love by charging forth into the external world, entering physical relationships, conquering and being conquered by the love in the physical environment and by the people in it. The Princess of Cups, on the other hand, learns inner love from her psychic internal world, her dreams, hopes, and fears, often fantasies, and by her natural inner strength of emotion.

Queens are nurturing their element. After the Princess has taken in the energy and the Prince has utilized it, the Queens take care of it. The Queens love the energy, nurture it, and protect it.

Kings manifest their element. After learning, utilizing, and nurturing the energy, the King orders it up. He is the person who makes things happen and manifests them in reality.

Kings and Queens both possess their element. Because the Princess has taken it in, and the Prince has expanded it, by the time it reaches the King and Queen they possess it. The Queen possesses her element on the inner level, and the King on the outer. Again, inner is defined as internal, an introvert; outer is defined as external, and an extravert. The Queen of Wands has self-confidence when dealing with the intuitive internal world, her inner strength and trust, and her perceptions in it. The King of Wands has self-confidence with the physical external world, his physical environment and the people in it. The Queen derives strength and joy from the internal world, and the King derives his strength and joy from the external world. Because Queens possess their element on an introverted level, they are able to nurture it for others on the inner level. Because Kings possess their element as extroverts, they are able to manifest it for others on an outer level. For we must first possess something as our own before we are able to give it away to others.

In effect, the Princess and Prince are two sides of a cube, and the King and Queen are the other two sides of the same cube.

The Prince and Princess learn it, so that as they grow, they can become the King and Queen who possess it.

In the tarot, Princesses and Queens are women. Usually, the Princess is the younger woman, and the Queen is more mature. Princes and Kings are men, the Prince being younger, and the King being the more mature man. In using the Myers-Briggs Type Indicator in conjunction with the court cards, this is not to insinuate that all introverts are women and all extraverts are men; nor that all people learning their element are young, and that people possessing their element are older. It does so happen that in many cases both are true, but the court cards are pictures attempting to express a personality type in one single card by one single picture. Considering all the voluminous material that could be written on a single personality type, the court cards have exceeded expectations in expressing the amount of information they do in a single picture, and we can applaud them because they have chosen the logical sex and age bracket to represent a certain personality type. As a matter of fact, it is almost inconceivable to imagine how some esoteric decks have managed to express so much of the essence of a singular archetypal behavior in one picture. Logically and statistically speaking the correspondences are uncanny. But then the longer you study the tarot, the more you discover that there is little about the tarot that isn't uncanny! It is a masterpiece of wondrous infinitudes always unfolding itself unto its perceiver.

COURT CARD DEFINITIONS

In the following summation of court cards, the titles used in the Golden Dawn system are given first. Then I list the court card's personality type. The first letter in parenthesis tells whether this person is an introvert or an extravert (I for Introvert and E for Extravert). The next two letters in parenthesis indicate the court card's superior and auxiliary functions (N for Intuition, F for Feeling, T for Thinking, and S for Sensation). The superior function is underlined to denote its dominance over the secondary auxiliary function, which is not. Sometimes the superior function is shown as the third letter and sometimes as the second letter because the preference is used differently with extraverts and introverts.

Note how the court card's MBTI superior function is exactly the same as the dominant element given by the Golden Dawn (i.e., Princess of Wands—Earth of *Fire*—I<u>N</u>FJ; Prince of Discs—Air of *Earth*—E<u>S</u>FP; Queen of Cups—Water of *Water*—IS<u>F</u>P). Yet the end of the Order of the Golden Dawn in 1902 and the beginning of the Myers-Briggs Type Indicator in the summer of 1942 were approximately 40 years apart, and supposedly not in any way related nor concerned with one another. The two groups may have even considered themselves as opposing factors if they had known about each other.

The last letter in parenthesis gives the card's type, Judging or Perceptive, J or P.

The whole personality is put together by the use of all four letters. For instance, the Princess of Wands is an I<u>N</u>FJ:

I Introvert
<u>N</u> Dominant function of Intuition
F Auxiliary function of Feeling
J Judging type

The third paragraph gives the key phrase for what the court card demonstrates. The fourth paragraph provides a few characteristics of the court card and a title most appropriate for its psychological type.

By reading some characteristics of the introvert and extravert and the judging and perceptive type given in this chapter, you may be able to ascertain to a slight degree what type you are. When attempting to ascertain your own personality type, it's best not to rely on personal judgment if possible. Most people are usually not at all who they think they are. For those who are interested in pursuing psychological typing, the

Myers-Briggs Type Indicator can now be taken through many local universities or humanistic psychologists. It has become extremely popular in academic quarters, and a phone call to one of these sources may give the reader additional information. Fortunately, there are now at least three excellent books available,[3] which have been written for the general public and are wonderfully helpful for determining your psychological type as well as the types that inhabit your environment.

PRINCESSES

Princess of Wands: The Princess of the Shining Flame; the Rose of the Palace of Fire; Princess and Empress of the Salamanders; Throne of the Ace of Wands. Earth of Fire.

Introverted intuition with feeling (INFJ).

Learning inner self-confidence.

THE FREE SPIRIT. Restless and irritable. Wanting to be free. Brings messages, telephone calls, news, information, a new acquaintance.

Princess of Cups: Princess of the Water and Lotus of the Palace of the Floods; Princess and Empress of Nymphs and Undines; Throne of the Ace of Cups. Earth of Water.

Introverted feeling with intuition. (INFP).

Learning inner love.

---

[3]The author wishes to refer the reader to three particularly good books on psychological typing: Otto Kroeger and Janet M. Thuesen, *Type Talk: The Sixteen Personality Types that Determine How We Live, Love & Work* (New York: Delacorte, 1989); David Keirsey and Marilyn Bates, *Please Understand Me: Character and Temperament Types* (Del Mar, CA: Prometheus Nemesis, 1978); and Isabel Briggs Myers, with Peter B. Myers, *Gifts Differing* (Palo Alto, CA: Consulting Psychologists Press, 1980).

THE DREAMER. Learning to love and to be loved again, sometimes after hurt and withdrawal. Brings messages from or about the psychic realm, dreams, and emotions.

Princess of Swords: Princess of the Rushing Winds; Lotus of the Palace of Air; Princess and Empress of the Sylphs and Sylphides; Throne of the Ace of Swords. Earth of Air.

Introverted thinking with intuition (INTP).

Learning inner intellect.

THE INITIATOR. Brings messages through or about the spoken or written word, through communication. Brings messages concerning a change.

Princess of Discs: Princess of Echoing Hills; Rose of the Palace of Earth; Princess and Empress of the Gnomes; Throne of the Ace of Pentacles. Earth of Earth.

Introverted sensing with feeling (ISFJ).

Learning inner security.

THE LEARNER. Needing to establish security. Study and introspection. Brings messages concerning health, money, work or study.

——————————— PRINCES ———————————

Prince of Wands: Prince of the Chariot of Fire; Prince and Emperor of the Salamanders. Air of Fire.

Extraverted intuition with feeling (ENFP).

Learning outer self-confidence.

THE CAREFREE SPIRIT. A sudden inspiration. Many possibilities. A succession of new ideas or projects, not any or all of them necessarily being completed.

Prince of Cups: Prince of the Chariot of the Waters; Prince and Emperor of Nymphs and Undines. Air of Water.

Extraverted feeling with intuition (ENFJ).

Learning outer love.

THE LOVER. Desiring one's soulmate. Harmonious human contacts and enjoyment in the qualities and companionship of others. Likely to develop strong loyalties through projections.

Prince of Swords: Prince of the Chariots of the Winds; Prince and Emperor of Sylphs and Sylphides. Air of Air.

Extraverted thinking with intuition. (ENTJ).

Learning outer intellect.

THE THINKER. Total focus and absorption in something. Organizes the facts. Analytical and impersonal. Evolving a frame-of-reference to base his personal truths on.

Prince of Discs: Prince of the Chariot of Earth; Prince and Emperor of the Gnomes. Air of Earth.

Extraverted sensing with feeling (ESFP).

Learning outer security.

THE BUILDER. Realistic learning from experience and life. Concerned with building a strong financial future.

——————————— QUEENS ———————————

Queen of Wands: Queen of the Thrones of Flame; Queen of the Salamanders or Salamandrines. Water of Fire.

Introverted intuition with thinking. (INTJ).

Possesses inner self-confidence.

THE SEER. Intensely individualistic. Motivated by inspiration and able to inspire confidence and courage in others. Gifted with a keen intuitive inner-sight into the deeper meaning of things. Encourages individuality in others and retains individuality for self.

Queen of Cups: Queen of the Thrones of the Waters; Queen of Nymphs and Undines. Water of Water.

Introverted feeling with sensing (IS_F_P).

Possesses inner love.

THE LISTENER. Being water so that another sees his own reflection in her; being the screen for other people's projections. Strong harmony in the inner life of feeling and able to give a deep inner nurturing to others. Not motivated by need for recognition or ego-acknowledgement and so is able to be devoted to others.

Queen of Swords: Queen of the Thrones of Air; Queen of the Sylphs and Sylphides. Water of Air.

Introverted thinking with sensing (IS_T_P).

Possesses inner intellect.

THE PROFESSIONAL. Handles situations capably, quickly and efficiently. Helps others with decisions and organizing and practical application. Often the real strength behind the organization.

Queen of Discs: Queen of the Thrones of the Earth; Queen of the Gnomes. Water of Earth.

Introverted sensing with thinking (IS_T_J).

Possesses inner security.

THE PROVIDER. Has a great sense of responsibility and duty. Likes routine and established work. This Queen has traditionally been called "the answer to prayers." She is the most practical of Queens, and because she possesses inner security, she is able to provide security for others.

KINGS

King of Wands: Lord of the Flame and of the Lightning; King of the Spirits of Fire; King of the Salamanders. Fire of Fire.

Extraverted intuition with thinking (ENTP).

Possesses outer self-confidence.

THE FULFILLER. Being happy and fulfilling a desire. Able to delegate responsibilities to others to obtain his own aim. A natural leader because he is perceptive of the views of others and has the ability to manifest his self-confidence in his actions and life.

King of Cups: Lord of the Waves and of the Waters; King of the Hosts of the Sea; King of Undines and Nymphs. Fire of Water.

Extraverted feeling with sensing (ESFJ).

Possesses outer love.

THE PLEASER. Feeling real good. Often has many people who love him and may be unaware of this. Manifests harmonious situations and feelings. Helps people with relationship problems. An excellent diplomat.

King of Swords: Lord of the Winds and Breezes; King of the Spirit of Air; King of Sylphs and Sylphides. Fire of Air.

Extraverted thinking with sensing (ESTJ).

Possesses outer intellect.

CHAPTER 10

The Minor Arcana

The card meanings described in this chapter indicate a number of different ways to express energy. Nearly always, the words in bold are the essence of the card. If this meaning isn't recognized right away, and it will be in most cases, then look deeply into the situation and its underlying nature will usually be found. This bold description is the dynamics of the archetypal blueprint, containing both the light and dark of its own symmetry. The remaining description either expands on the general sense or presents applications which might apply in certain situations.

The Aces of each suit always relate to new conceptions before the beginning. When you receive an Ace in a reading you are going to have to do something. Not this instant–because Aces denote conceptions that are just being born–but you will have to do something soon. An Ace means that something is currently on its way to physical manifestation.

Aces also can be used as timing and direction cards. In a spread, if the Ace of Discs is laid out in a question pertaining to timing, the timing will be around December 21st. Allow a reasonable time span either before or after December 21st, keeping in mind that it will be closer to the Winter Solstice than to one of the other seasons. If the question is pertaining to direction, and the Ace of Discs is laid out, the direction will be to, or from, the North.

———————— WANDS OF POWER ————————

Ace of Wands – The Root of the Powers of Fire.[1] *Evokes the Force. Unseen self-organizing. The Self rising up from within. I want.* Strength, fortitude, enthusiasm, will, courage, and trust. Spiritual. The beginning of a new passion or desire. The beginning of new creativity or a career. Spring (0 Aries) March 21st. South.

2 of Wands – The Lord of Dominion. *Self-confidence.* Affirming and validating the self. Feeling good or not feeling good about yourself.

3 of Wands – The Lord of Established Strength. *Expressing yourself.* Negotiations. Striving to turn a dream into a reality. Or being uncertain of yourself.

4 of Wands – The Lord of Perfected Work. *Inactivity.* Achievement. Reaching a stage of satisfaction. Manifesting self-satisfaction. Feeling good about your situation. Wanting to have and hold on to more time and space for yourself.

5 of Wands – The Lord of Strife. *Being scattered. Activity.* Being busy. Sometimes too much activity, leaving little time, but sometimes just the right amount of activity. Seemingly outside occurrences interfering with your time or goals. Excitement and adventures.

6 of Wands – The Lord of Victory. *Stability.* A goal reached. Trusting and flowing with one's higher self. Depth of prayer or any form of concentration.

---

[1]The titles for the cards are taken from Robert Wang, *An Introduction to The Golden Dawn Tarot* (York Beach, ME: Samuel Weiser, Inc., 1987), pp. 64–66. From original documents on tarot from the Hermetic Order of the Golden Dawn, Book "T" – The Tarot.

7 of Wands – The Lord of Valour. *Slowdown.* Challenge. Fear. A sense of helplessness or hopelessness. Being thrown into physical reality or survival and having to rely upon instinct rather than intuition. Inaction in the midst of difficulties. Checking things out first.

8 of Wands – The Lord of Swiftness. *Charging forward. The end of delay.* Expanding your horizons. Activities and energy being released. Being almost there. Infatuation or falling in love.

9 of Wands – The Lord of Great Strength. *Persistence. Hanging in there.* Obtaining trust and know-how in your own perceptions and being comfortable with them. Expectation of change. Recovery from illness. Good health.

10 of Wands – The Lord of Oppression. *Energy in extreme.* Responsibilities and duties. Being full of fire, passion, intuition. Transformation of inner. *Joie de vivre.*

If wand people choose conscious survival to the point of excluding unconscious intuition, they can find themselves burdened with excessive physical responsibilities or dull regulated routine which they have unwittingly brought on themselves. Wands are not comfortable with anything that takes away freedom or ties them down excessively. On the other hand, if wands have flowed with their intuition, the 10 of Wands is a richly fulfilling experience.

--------------------- CUPS OF LOVE ---------------------

Ace of Cups – The Root of the Powers of Water. *Channels the Force. Absorption and assimilation. Emotions or love rising up from within. I feel.* The beginning of new emotions or feelings. In a layout, an enhancement of other good influences or a mitigating power over bad ones. Falling in love. Summer (0 Cancer) – June 21st. East.

2 of Cups – The Lord of Love. *Inner peace. Love.* A relationship. A healing union of opposites. Being wounded by the knowledge of your own love. An engagement. A romance. A marriage.

3 of Cups – The Lord of Abundance. *Experiencing feelings. Expanded emotions.* Friendship. Grace. Or being uncertain about a relationship.

4 of Cups –The Lord of Blended Pleasure. *Receiving pleasure and success mixed with slight discomfort.* Boredom. Not being ready to let go of a relationship. Maybe being slightly bored but feeling the attributes outweigh the drawbacks.

5 of Cups – The Lord of Loss in Pleasure. *Changes in emotion. Feeling disassembled.* Disappointment. Sadness. Ending a relationship or entering a new and perhaps more satisfying phase in a current one.

6 of Cups – The Lord of Pleasure. *Harmony. The natural flow of psychic energy. Sense of well-being.* Subtlety of feelings and understanding of surrounding conditions. Energy flowing to and fro according to what is given and received. All light goes to all dark; all dark goes to all light; half dark goes to half light, and back again. The brighter the light, the darker the shadow.

7 of Cups – The Lord of Illusionary Success. *The card of choice. A choice will have to be made.* A mystical vision or experience. Intemperance – the inability, perhaps temporary, to combine emotion and imagination. Or preparing to combine opposites on the inner before they combine on the outer.

8 of Cups – The Lord of Abandoned Success. *Leaving behind the known for the unknown. Getting your act together.* Taking a direction in the spheres of emotion. Progressing to affections or feelings which are new and different, or somehow changed.

9 of Cups – The Lord of Material Happiness. *The card of "wishes fulfilled."* When it appears in a layout, a wish will be fulfilled. Receiving what one has yearned for. Generally a happy card.

10 of Cups – The Lord of Perfected Success. *Being full of emotion.* Being grateful. Being gratified to or beyond capacity. Perhaps someone loves you and takes care of you, providing unquestionable and lasting security. Being full of any emotion.

———————————— SWORDS ————————————

Ace of Swords – The Root of the Powers of Air. *Changes the force. Expansion and celebration. Change rising up from within. I think.* The beginning of new information or a problem. This is a most paradoxical card, and very much depends upon the person involved. This can be a card of celebration or a card of dire consequences. No matter how the card is interpreted, it is a card of change. It denotes that a build-up has taken place in the unconscious which soon must expand or explode into the conscious. Autumn (0 Libra) – September 23rd. West.

2 of Swords – The Lord of Peace Restored. *Acceptance. Agreement.* The intellect agrees, perhaps temporarily, with the natural course of action, or with the heart. Two opposing forces set one against the other to achieve balance. Not choosing the one over the other, for choosing one implies the loss of the other. This is choosing neither – the middle, or third alternative, which achieves a satisfactory balance.

3 of Swords – The Lord of Sorrow. *Indecision. Mental strife.* When one is forced to make a mental choice between two or more possible options, and the mind wants to make one choice, but the heart wants to make the other choice. In this case, it is important to go with the heart even though the mind doesn't agree.

4 of Swords – The Lord of Rest from Strife. *Rest and recovery.* Sometimes this card is a rest from mental or other strife which has been causing mental strain. It can denote illness, forcing the person to rest and recover. Whatever the person experiences, it will bring a sort of mental stabilization, sometimes in the most unexpected way and when one least expects it. The intellect relinquishes its control.

5 of Swords – The Lord of Defeat. *Mental turmoil. Problems with shifting viewpoints.* The need to accept the inevitable. A need to change what you thought was previously correct. Or a time of great mental activity and exercise.

6 of Swords – The Lord of Earned Success. *Balance. Overview.* The power of safe passage from one world to another. The mind watching itself. Development of full consciousness. Great mental stability. Travel. A trip or journey.

7 of Swords – The Lord of Unstable Effort. *Avoiding confrontation. Sneaking around. Futility.* The mind may be taking in information that it is yet unable to express on the outer. New plans and preparation being laid in the mind, but it is not yet clearly seen how to arrive at completion. The mind confused between intellect and illusion.

8 of Swords – The Lord of Shortened Force. *Interference.* The mind arrives at pure individual reason. A light dawns, and the intellect knows how to proceed. Or there is too much stimulation and information coming in, causing a momentary mental maze.

9 of Swords – The Lord of Despair and Cruelty. *Mental conclusion. The solution to a mental problem. The shadow.* Disappointment in wishes. Illness. Insomnia. Arriving at a solution or answer to a mental concern or bothersome problem.

10 of Swords – The Lord of Ruin. *No choice but to let go. Final ending.* A crisis point, total exhaustion, no more hope left, a critical point reached when there is no choice but to let go.

A 10 of Swords situation results from a build-up of intense and prolonged energy in the psyche over a long period of time. This can be positive, as in the case of being in turmoil over a mental problem for so long that the person no longer has any choice but to let go of it, and this letting go results in immediate relief, an answer often suddenly materializes.

If the psyche is unable to deal with pressure, the 10 of Swords can be negative. Discs (sensation) may become physically ill; wands (intuitive) depressed, unmotivated, and listless; and cups (feeling) may experience nightmares, paranoia, or anger. Swords, on the other hand, are usually quite comfortable with their own element, and often experience this as just one more crisis to take charge of. The 10 of Swords is generally thought of as an unhappy card, but it can bring answers, new insight, and great relief. As Carl Jung said, "It is from need and distress that new forms of existence arise, and not from idealistic requirements or mere wishes."[2]

--- DISCS ---

Ace of Discs – The Root of the Powers of Earth. *Grounds the force. Remembering and memory. The rising up of physical or material resolve and clarity from within. I do.* The beginning of new money, work, financial or material well-being – any new physical form or pattern. Winter (0 Capricorn) – December 21st. North.

2 of Discs – The Lord of Harmonious Change. *Daily living. Harmony of juggling and interaction of dualities.* Handling two or more

---

[2]Carl Jung, quoted in Stephan A. Hoeller, *The Gnostic Jung and the Seven Sermons to the Dead* (Wheaton, IL: Theosophical Publishing House, 1982), p. 137.

situations. Opposites are not the opposite ends of a line or polar opposites; they are the two halves of a circle, each one becoming the other. Yin and Yang.

3 of Discs – The Lord of Material Works. *Working. Increase.* Producing. Effort and hard work enjoyed by strength of purpose. Or doubts caused by the inability to be flexible.

4 of Discs – The Lord of Earthly Power. *Not wanting to let go. Protecting. Mine, mine, mine!!!* Possessing something of value to yourself and not wanting to let go. This can be anything – a way of life, solitude, peace, habits, etc.

5 of Discs – The Lord of Material Trouble. *Anxiety. Worry.* A time when calming repetitious routine is disrupted. Being busy with many physical activities and worrying about how to handle it all. Or small annoying mishaps and delays occurring.

6 of Discs – The Lord of Material Success. *Energy exchange. Steadiness in realization.* Giving and/or receiving gifts or resources. Having enough health and physical energy or resources in yourself to be able to include others.

7 of Discs – The Lord of Success Unfulfilled. *Delay. Waiting.* Demotivation. No inspiration. Being bound to earthly conditions for a while. Unable to take physical action. Things not going as you wish. Being thwarted from your desires. Or taking time out to re-evaluate your physical goals. Going back and redoing something. Evaluating something in danger of too much crystallization, resulting from being confused between crystallization and endurance.

8 of Discs – The Lord of Prudence. *Learning.* Using your skills in ways which are satisfactory or profitable. Utilizing your talents on earth, or learning to use your talents for future profit. Utilizing your own natural knowledge or creativity for its own reward. Can be gain of money in small sums.

9 of Discs – The Lord of Material Gain. *Love of work made visible.* Love of nature. Enjoyment of what you are doing. Solitary creative work. Unexpected money.

10 of Discs – The Lord of Wealth. *Financial security. Feeling secure.* Group or family support. A charm of power, bringing protection and security. Inheritance. Happy family. Warm family. Someone may be providing lasting financial security for you. Reaping rewards from doing what you love. The 10 of Discs can also be being totally overwhelmed with a physical condition, i.e., work overload or physical burnout.

• • •

Whether any card will be experienced positively or negatively depends upon the individual and upon the surrounding cards. A materially-oriented wand person who is not working at what he loves isn't likely to find much joy in the 9 of Wands, whereas a wand person expressing creativity (whether bringing financial rewards or not) is likely to be very happy in the 9 of Wands.

When you work with these card interpretations, apply the meaning of the number to the essence of the suit. Take, for example, the 10 of Cups. If all 10's mean being full of the element, and all cups are emotions, feelings, the psychic realm, all conditions dealing with "heart openings," then receiving the 10 of Cups must mean being "full of emotion." When interpreting the 10 of Cups, it can indicate an actual physical relationship you are involved in, or it can mean an inner relationship that you are having with the Higher Self. Perhaps you are deeply involved in a love affair with the universe or with life. It can even mean being full of feeling for a fantasy image. For cups, the inner realms are sometimes as real, or more real, than the physical realm; for some cups, fantasies are larger than life. On the other hand, the 10 of cups can also mean being full of sadness, sorrow, or grief. But no matter what the specific interpretation, receiving the 10 of Cups always implies being *full* of emotion — even though that can be *any* emotion. In all the Minor Arcana interpretations, the meaning of the number should be combined with the dynamics of the suit to arrive at the particular card's meaning.

If it seems that meanings of the same number of different suits are contradictory or not related, this is because numbers do mean different things to different suits. As previously mentioned in the chapter on court cards, all people have a superior function (or suit) plus an inferior function. Our superior function is what we are happy with and what we have brought into consciousness, so we experience our superior and auxiliary functions usually most pleasantly. On the other hand, all people also have an inferior function, which is always the opposite of our superior. The inferior function is what we have suppressed into unconsciousness, what we don't acknowledge in ourselves, usually resulting in negative expressions arising from these suits.

The superior function is *always* opposite the inferior function:

Superior	Inferior
swords	cups
cups	swords
wands	discs
discs	wands

In other words, this list tells us that disc people are likely to enjoy the suit of their own superior function, discs, and have trouble with the inferior suit of wands. Wand people are likely to identify greatly with and vastly enjoy the suit of wands, but have difficulty identifying with discs. The superior and inferior functions are important to understand because they tell us what we are likely to experience positively and negatively when we do readings; with this knowledge predictions can become a breeze.

For example, a 3 of Swords to sword people is not the same as the 3 of Swords to cup people, and they experience it very differently. A sword may not have much difficulty with the 3 of Swords because the 3 of Swords means being torn between emotion and logic. Because sword people's superior function is swords (thinking) and their inferior function is cups (feeling), they aren't likely to experience much conflict when they receive the 3 of Swords because emotions don't normally concern them particularly. However, when cups experience the 3 of Swords, we have a totally different story. The rise of logic, or the thinking function, as represented by the 3 of Swords, can cause emotional turmoil brought on by the eruption of logic—a function that cups are not comfortable with. This is not to imply this is the only way to interpret this card, but each card needs to be looked at from the viewpoint of the people involved in the reading. We all possess different and unique relationships among our own personal functions and will behave and respond accordingly. Knowing the superior, auxiliary, and inferior functions helps determine how people will respond and react to a reading or to a certain card, and helps us determine whether or not people will see something as good or bad.

The superior function (and thus, also the inferior function) can be determined by a number of ways. You can use the (MBTI) Myers-Briggs Type Indicator—this is probably the best and most valid method. The superior function can also be determined using astrology. In astrology, the superior function is determined by the ruler of the Sun in the natal chart, i.e., if the Sun is in Virgo, the Sun's ruler is Mercury. If Mercury is in a fire sign (Aries, Leo, or Sagittarius), then the superior function is intuition. If the Sun is in Aries, the Sun's ruler is Mars. If Mars is in a fire sign, then the superior function is intuition. If the Sun is in Aquarius, the ruler is Uranus. If Uranus is in an earth sign, then the superior function is sensation. The element that rules the person's Sun is usually the superior function. Since the inferior function is always opposite the superior function, by locating the superior function in a chart through the above method, one automatically knows the inferior function.

We can also determine functions by choosing the correct court card. The success of this method depends largely upon the skills and knowledge of the reader and should be approached with the utmost caution. Sometimes we choose the court card we would like to be, rather than the one we actually are.

If you memorize the list of synonymous definitions from the chapter on the four suits, all of this becomes clear and orderly. The list is repeated below:

Wands	Clubs	Fire	Intuition
Cups	Hearts	Water	Feeling
Swords	Spades	Air	Thinking
Discs	Diamonds	Earth	Sensation

If these words are understood, and we realize that the same laws and actions apply to each, the concepts can be applied to determine a person's functions. These same four elements also apply to the suits, the court cards, the Minor Arcana and the Major Arcana. The tarot is constant. The four elements filter through with the sureness of all wholes that contain the same code-pattern in their parts as the whole that contains the same identical code pattern in its singularity.

THE LIGHT AND DARK SIDES OF CARDS

Beginning students of tarot need to understand that no suit, number, or card is all bad. Given enough time, slowly but firmly the cards will persevere and show us the light of their darkness and the darkness of their light. They are like The Hierophant saying, "See this." And if we try, we eventually will.

Every number, suit, and card contains within itself both its negative *and* its positive symbolism. Nevertheless, certain cards or, in the case of the Swords, an entire suit is sometimes thought of in a negative light. The cards that follow are among those that seem to get the most bad press.

In many decks the Sword suit depicts people being stabbed, hung, choked, mutilated, or being disposed of in some similarly unpleasant fashion. It's enough to make your hair stand on end and make the more timid tremble with trepidation.

There are several reasons why swords usually end up with a bad reputation. One reason is that they rule change, and who among us likes change? We may say we do, and even at times find ourselves wishing for it, but when it comes down to actual *real* change, most of us do not exactly relish it.

Another reason Swords are shunned is because they deal with logical mind processes. The swords' superior function is thinking, or the conscious mind, which means the unconscious is virtually unexplored territory to most swords. Though unknown to all of us, the unconscious is especially ignored by swords. Because swords are not in touch with their emotional subconscious, they typically try to express their emotions through logic or the physical, which just doesn't allow for emotions and intuition. Consequently, swords often tend to try to cure one crisis by creating another.

If told they are unaware of the unconscious, they may flatly deny it. Or if we speak of educated swords, they may outwardly agree with you, but usually they are unaware that they have not transferred awareness from the mind to the heart. Swords don't know how to do this; they have to learn. After all, like all unconscious functions in all people, it is *un*conscious. But the unconscious is a psychic process and one which must be *experienced*, thus it cannot be intellectualized. This is where swords have problems, for they often intellectualize, and find the secret realm of their emotions and psyche (and everyone else's) unknown and hidden.

Another reason Swords may be the most difficult suit is because our Western civilization at present consists mainly of extraverted thinking, sensation, and thirdly, feeling people.

Men are most inclined toward the thinking (sword) function,[3] and men generally establish, maintain, and enforce the rules of the society. Hence the body and the mind are given credence and value in our society. Intuition and feeling are often looked upon as unwanted and unnecessary stepchildren. Feeling is relegated to the sphere of the "weak" female, "wimpy" male, or "immature" child. Intuition is either scoffed at, denied, ridiculed, or ignored altogether (although it has, on numerous occasions, also been burned at the stake). Many people so closely identify with their minds and bodies that they now believe these make up their total being. People have turned to the church for religious answers, to the government for social answers, to the patriarchal family for emotional answers, and to the material for physical answers. Swords and discs are, in effect, ruling the day.

It is through the discs' physical function that swords express intellectual function. Both functions are in trouble because of the denial of their complimentary processes. We could write volumes on the physical breakdown resulting—everything from the dissolution of the ozone and the crash of world stock markets to the advent of AIDS. Aches, pains, operations, disease, birth defects, and old age infirmity run rampant. The advantage of the physical, however, is that our Earth, Mother Nature, is also a visible and viable power. Swords are powerful, too, but the difference is Swords indicate an energy that is incapable of acknowledging something not concrete and visible. When swords gain the upper hand they have no awareness or ability to perceive their role in pre-destined and unavoidable destruction. They have not the slightest inkling why addictions, suicides, violence and corruption are running rampant, and in typical sword fashion, instead of acknowledging these as all too obvious results of a denial of feeling and intuition, swords attempt to

---

[3]Based on an early unpublished study by Isabel Briggs Myers: "Western civilization has inclined men toward thinking, women toward feeling, and both sexes toward extraversion and judging attitude . . . . In the general population, there may be three extraverts to every introvert and three sensing types to every intuitive" (Isabel Briggs Myers, with Peter B. Myers, *Gifts Differing*, p. 190).

fight with the only thing they know — more discs and swords. I mean they repair the body instead of the soul. They foster the illusion of intellect instead of encouraging the development of intuition.

FIVES

Fives. Yuk! Fives! Lives there a reader among us who looks favorably upon the fives? Who wants to see our hard-earned energy scattered and dissipated? Yet in the five we can be active, finally get off our duffs to do something! Many tarot teachers say that fives, sevens, swords, certain cups, certain wands, etc., bring us growth through their pain, and isn't that, oh so lovely, and that if these cards bring us pain now, we will have growth later. Yeah, and if my aunt had wheels she'd be a scooter.

No card has to symbolize pain. Yes, sometimes a so-called negative card indicates pain, but sometimes so does the Ace of Wands, and 2 of Cups, the 9 of Discs, the 9 of Cups, and so on.

SEVENS

Sevens. Oh dear, here we go again. Who wants a seven? Not me. Yet the seven can be encountering our deepest inner yearnings, our most exciting dreams, coming to realize the answers to questions we've been searching for from the ace through the six. It can indicate taking time off, kicking off our shoes, leaning back, and taking a load off our feet. It can indicate seeing things for the first time that we've never noticed were there before and wondering at our blindness. The seven is deep, yes, and deep is beautiful.

TENS

Think of the 10 of Swords. It sends a quiet little shudder down our spines. And yet, it is during the 10 of Swords that we can achieve some of our greatest intentions. And I don't mean after the 10, or from the great pain caused during the 10, but because of the 10 of Swords in its essence — right then and there — when it is presently doing its thing. Swords indicate knowledge; they symbolize energy expanding and celebrating itself. What we take in through the cups is released through the swords, and it can be a beautiful process. By the time we go through the first nine steps of the swords and reach the 10, our accumulated energy can explode into a universal cascade of drive, energy, and will. For surely, if swords have anything, they have will. Swords can indicate finally reaching our goals—being full of purpose and honor and creation. In the 10 of Swords we can create what we have learned through the first nine swords. So the 10 can indicate an adventure not before lived, a dream manifesting itself into reality, a wish come true!

When I see a new tarot book I always check the description for the 10 of Wands. Ten to one (excuse the pun) it will read, "10 of Wands = oppression, drudgery, and general Woe is Me!" And yet, a ten is being full of the element. A ten is the total of all nine cards preceding it. A wand is fire, spirit, and unseen organizing. How joyful it is to receive a 10 of Wands when it is the fulfillment of spirit and fire! There is no other high quite like it, for the spirit leaps with fire and flame and feels itself in touch with its Higher Self that creates from its hidden unseen organizing. In the 10 of Wands is the phenomenon that our expectations are at last fulfilled.

•   •   •

And then there are the bright light cards. These are the cards that only have lovely descriptions. There are certain cards that can only bring good news and happy tidings regardless of anything else. But if we think about it, logic tells us that we will forever only reap what we sow, one way or the other. Logic tells us that every up has its down, every yin its yang, every day its night. It is an illusion that there can be pleasure without pain, reward without effort.

Ever hear a bad word about the Ace of Cups? Well, aces are conceptions and cups are feeling, and just as the Ace of Cups can conceive feelings of love and tender emotion, it can also conceive feelings of hatred and bitterness. In the Ace of Cups a conception is a conception, and an emotion is an emotion, and the archetype does not distinguish. It is, by universal law, drawn to its likeness, whatever that may be.

Consider the 10 of Discs. We all want to hear that we are going to receive an inheritance or at the very least, be protected financially. Barring that grace, we expect everlasting security from the 10 of Discs, or so the books say. But again, tens indicate being full of the element, and discs are material and physical realization—work, and money. If people want to have a real bummer trip, they can try on the 10 of Discs when it means being so full of the physical and material that they are up to their chins in money, demands, money, responsibilities, money, worry, money, tension, money, headaches, money, illness, money, anxiety, money, board meetings, money, dissatisfied customers and employees, money, and well, you get the picture. And let us not forget that discs rule the physical body and health. The 10 of Discs isn't all brightness when it means being full of sickness, full of disease, or full of pain.

Keep in mind that every card is the whole of its parts, both darkness and light, and remember that the archetypes represented in the cards are not coming to reward or to punish. They are not concerned with individual personalities but simply attract and are attracted to the fulfillment of their and our destinies.

CHAPTER 11

The Major Arcana

The Druids did not, and it is said they still don't, believe in written communication. When it comes to describing the tarot, especially the Major Arcana, one can certainly see why. The Druids feel that under most circumstances the written word hinders the effort to inform, and this is why priests pass down the teachings orally. It is very difficult to describe the Major Arcana. I have tried to catch the essence of the major archetypes without burdening them with specific examples. The brief descriptions given are a barebones endeavor to show only a few of the possible expressions.

Because archetypes are infinite circles whose centers are everywhere and circumferences nowhere, they cannot be limited to only this or that. They are smaller wholes within the larger whole.

In spite of knowing better, we cannot help but feel that certain expressions of an archetype are bad, while others are good. We try to overcome this by labeling what we perceive as polarities, passive and aggressive, light and dark, yin and yang, but definition will forever and always be flavored by individual value judgments as to what personally affects us as either good or bad. It seems it can't be helped. Knowing that good and evil are relative, and knowing that just because we have named something does not mean we understand it, we can now move through the descriptions of the Major Arcana without taking anything too literally.

Even though it is not feasible to determine which tiny specific portion of the archetype will manifest physically (other than in exceptional magical moments of divination, and even then we cannot be absolutely certain until afterward when we are blessed with the complacent gift of hindsight), it is possible to ascertain certain patterns and processes that will be activated by becoming familiar with the archetype's synchronicities as displayed through the physical plane, dreams, hunches, thoughts, ideas, knowledge, and other forms of human perception. It is this and learning how it applies in our lives that is a large portion of the art of reading cards.

•   •   •

The following section describes the twenty-two cards of the Major Arcana. The archetype's title is the one used by the Golden Dawn. The astrological sign or planet is listed next so readers can see the astrological equivalent of the card. By comparing the card with its astrological function, we can expand comprehension of both tarot and astrology because they compliment each other while maintaining rather different expressions of the same vibration.

The letters on the cards are derived from the twenty-two letters of the Hebrew alphabet. We can associate the numbers of the twenty-two Major Arcana with the Hebrew alphabet because Hebrew letters are also numbers. When working with symbolism of the Qabalistic Tree of Life (a mystical study of Judaism), each Hebrew letter also represents a letter of the alphabet, a word in the Hebrew language, and a number. From these symbols, other symbols are also interpreted, such as color, sound, tone, form, etc. The simple letters are attributed to the twelve signs of the zodiac and their corresponding activities. The double letters are attributed to the seven planets and are so called because each is seen to contain its own polarity. The maternal letters are attributed to the three elements of fire, earth, and air; Spirit not being attributed because it is above all these, or *is* all these.

The phrase that describes each card shows the light essence of the archetype. Most assuredly these phrases can be one-sided in their translations, i.e., Arcanum VI, Lovers, can mean "Going Apart" just as much as it can mean "Coming Together," but hopefully, the phrase catches the concept behind the code-principle as expressed in its more positive origin and structure.

I have also included a section on expressions that are commonly heard when the archetype is activated. These are what people might be heard to say when the archetype is around and doing its thing. Some of these expressions are funny and it is often in humor that we find our greater truths. A wise man once said, "If it isn't close to laughter, it isn't close to God."

The description also includes titles for the cards that have been used in a traditional way, and some modern titles are included as well. They are included because the oldest titles, like their cards, have much to say, and some of the newer titles, such as those by Aleister Crowley and Gareth Knight, also touch on an important aspect of the archetype.

When you get a card in a reading, you'll need to know how to interpret it. The more positive polarity of the archetype has been emphasized because it's more fun (and healthy) to be positive. When you receive a card in a reading and don't experience the archetype as you expect, it is usually the case that the card has manifested in your life, but in another area or in a different form than you expected. For instance, if you receive The Empress in a reading, you may expect it to manifest as the soulmate you've always been searching for. Instead, you may get a new goldfish! Or a family member, or close friend, or stranger may unexpectedly show you an act of love that startles you into a deeper knowledge of what love is really all about. But receiving The Empress in a reading means that love, nurturing, giving—some process of the number 3—will be experienced. And it may not be in the form of our *receiving* love but rather us *giving* love.

Whenever we receive a certain card in a reading, it is well to remember that the archetype is doing its thing—not ours. If we get The Magician and don't recognize any coincidences popping up in our lives, The Magician doesn't care. He puts the coincidence there all right, but it's up to us to spot it. Should we get Justice and become ill in spite of the fact that in our opinion there's no reason for it, we can rest assured there is. That is one reason why the tarot is such an excellent learning and self-growth tool—it tells us the way things are whether we are consciously aware of them or not. Archetypes are not influenced by our conscious recognition of them, so any time we have trouble recognizing how a certain card is playing out in our lives, we might do well to take its unconscious word for it before we rely on our conscious word against it.

0 · THE FOOL

Golden Dawn Title: The Spirit of The Aether

Astrological Planet: Uranus

Maternal Letter: Air-Spiritual

Phrase: Trusting silence

Expressions: Shhhh.
Gulp.
Uh, oh.
Whoops.
He was here a minute ago.
Famous last words!
Look out be-l-o-w-w-w!

Other Titles: The Mad One; The Beggar; Misery; The Crocodile

Key: The Trickster; the Shadow; ignorance; silence; being unaware; plunging into the unknown; protection through faith or innocence.

The Fool is human. The one who kills. Madness. What we do not recognize as our own we project out into our environment and onto others. He is what we are unaware of in ourselves. "If you bring forth what is within you, what you bring forth will save you. If you do not bring forth what is within you, what you do not bring forth will destroy you."[1]

The Fool can be the circumference without the center, when hundreds of fragments come so fast and disharmoniously from the circumference that there is no control for lack of a center. It is chaos. In this case there is no question of one exercising free will. Free will is not possible unless one first possesses a center. The Fool can be a situation or a circumstance in life that is about to occur and we are not conscious of it yet. He is that which cannot be helped, that which will take care of itself, that over which we apparently have no control.

The Fool has been called "The Lord of Silence" because in our Higher Self he expresses the true idea of Silence. He is our Will at its best, which issues forth to meet every challenge, expanding or contracting to accommodate whatever human situation life offers. The perfect Fool is one who is always fluid, varying his form to concur with whatever imperfection it encounters. If The Fool is met with fluidity and strength, he brings purity by his very nature of Silence, or Nothing, so that he is beyond all intellection or intuition. If he is met with fear and limitation, he is the Trickster.

When receiving The Fool in a reading, there is something afoot in your life of which you are unaware. You should be prepared for the unexpected because anything can happen.

---

[1]Elaine Pagels, *The Gnostic Gospels* (New York: Vintage Books/Random House, 1981), p. 152.

I · THE MAGICIAN

Golden Dawn Title: The Magus of Power

Astrological Planet: Mercury

Double Letter: Life-Death

Phrase: Doing it anyway

Expressions: I'm winging it.
What a coincidence!
Is this your idea of some kind of joke?
Now you see it—now you don't.
Believe it or not!

Other Titles: The Juggler; The Magus

Key: Origination; the word; learning; taking in energy; unity; active magic; synchronicity; manifestation of the spirit; ulterior arrangement of the abstract.

The Magician is energy sent forth—the Messenger of the Gods. In mythology, he was deemed by Jupiter to bring Jupiter's messages to people. Because the use of speech and writing distorts the Word of the Gods, manifestation implies illusion. Attempts to interpret are useless because all images are but similar manifestations of higher truths. The Magician regards the world as an excellent practical joke, but recognizes that the Gods are serious. His sole business is to transmit the messages of life from the Gods, and he is concerned with nothing else.

The Magician is continuous creation and perpetual motion, so statis contradicts the card. There are planes where duality is not perceived and perceptions where there are no dualities. The Magician is duality, and he is aware of this. He knows that all things are contained in all things. This being so, what can he lose? He can only gain.

When you get this card in a reading look for a synchronicity. Something will occur that looks like a coincidence but is really a manifestation of The Magician involved in the ulterior arrangement of the abstract archetype. Pay attention to the synchronicity to see what it may be showing you. If you don't know what it means, trying to figure it out may lead to answering a question you have or solving a problem you are puzzling over.

—————— II · THE HIGH PRIESTESS ——————

Golden Dawn Title: The Princess of the Silver Star

Astrological Planet: Moon

Double Letter: Peace-War

Phrase: Listening to your inner self

Expressions: Are you talking to me?
Who said that?
Say what?
Come again?
Can you please repeat that?
Are you kidding me?

Other Titles: The Female Pope; The Gate of the Sanctuary

Key: Creation; silent knowledge; utilizing energy; the law of analogy; anima—life; unconscious intuitive teaching, the tarot; awareness of Higher Self; binary; water/inner love.

Combining woman and God. To go within is to go without. To go without is to go within. To trust in the inner self means that the outer self shall be wholly taken care of. A magnet doesn't concern itself with what it attracts. It simply attracts what it is. The High Priestess is unconscious, which if it is but itself—calm, clear and bright—cannot attract any other than what it is and what is right. If one strives for self-awareness at all times, at each moment, constantly asking, "Is this what I am? Is this what I want?" and is able to answer yes, the Law of Analogy becomes conscious. "What is below is similar [NOT EQUAL] [*sic*] to what is above, and what is above is similar to what is below in order to ensure the perpetuation of the miracles of the Unique Thing."[2]

When you get The High Priestess in a reading, it is time to listen to your hunches and intuition and dreams. The High Priestess reaches us through the anima—that feminine part that symbolizes inner wisdom, serene inner knowing, and receptivity. Be aware of your unconscious intuitive signals and messages.

III · THE EMPRESS

Golden Dawn Title: The Daughter of the Mighty Ones

Astrological Planet: Venus

Double Letter: Wisdom-Folly

Phrase: Experiencing love

Expressions: Will you marry me?
It only hurts when I laugh.
There's no place like home.
She's stuck to him like cold oatmeal on a spoon.
He's all over her like white on rice.

Other Titles: The Grandmother; The Queen; Isis Urania

Key: Formation; nurturing energy; the law of attraction; taking care of; mother—the matrix, form, container; reproduction; nurturing and healing; love; allurement; abundance; Earth/physical love.

Because energy is "love" it flows by allurement, or gravity, or attraction; it flows in the direction of what it loves. It is The

---

[2]Mouni Sadhu's free translation of the classical Latin translation of the Emerald Tablets of Hermes Trismegistus, from Sadhu's *The Tarot* (North Hollywood, CA: Wilshire Book Co., 1968), p. 44.

Empress who bridges the gap between the world of inspiration (High Priestess) and the world of logic and science (Emperor). Whereas The High Priestess combines woman and God, The Empress combines woman and man. In this sense God means the Spirit, the "man" means the physical human being. Here are some comparisons to help clarify the likeness and unlikeness of the two:

High Priestess	Empress
The Virgin	The Royal Queen
Serves the Spirit	Fulfills the Spirit
Patience	Action
Passive waiting	Completion
Ruled by love	Rules by love
Guards something old	Reveals something new
Brings Spirit to inner reality	Brings Spirit to outer reality
Spiritual nurturing	Physical nurturing
The unattainable Mother	The attainable Mother
Water	Earth
Spiritual love	Physical love

It is The Empress who gives forth love in earth form, making it possible for us to experience it in physical manifestation. In other words, we learn to love the Earth and its inhabitants by being inhabitants ourselves.

> We become what we are aware of, and
> We become aware of what we love.
> That is why Love is the Force.
> That is why Love is the glue.

In a reading, The Empress usually indicates a love experience. She reveals something new in the way of receiving and/or giving love.

——————— IV · THE EMPEROR ———————

Golden Dawn Title: Son of the Morning; Chief among the Mighty

Astrological Sign: Aries

Simple Letter: Sight

Phrase: Making it happen

Expressions: What a pig! Or, What a man!
Get on your mark—get set—go!
Hi, yo, Silver!
Get the lead out.
Actions speak louder than words.
Just call me Action Jackson for your satisfaction.
Gentlemen—start your engines.

Other Titles: The Grandfather; The King; The Cubic Stone

Key: Expression, ordering energy; authority; form; realization; Father—dynamism; energy.

Combining man and woman. The basic necessity of form, for without form there is not realization. Manifestation appears in physical form *after* is has been prepared in advance on the inner.

When you get The Emperor in a reading, it means you're doing something and releasing energy in a physical form. He is energy on the physical plane—getting the job done. He nearly always represents action and sometimes intense activity. Your goals are usually fairly clear because The Emperor rules by reason and logic, law and established order. He can indicate action as a road to fulfillment, ordering up and releasing energy that you previously felt was inert or unexpressible. Or he can be someone in your environment whom you allow to play out this energy for you. Whichever, The Emperor in a reading means you're going to express or encounter that energy now in a very viable and concrete form.

——————— V · THE HIEROPHANT ———————

Golden Dawn Title: The Magus of the Eternal

Astrological Sign: Taurus

Simple Letter: Hearing

Phrase: Continuing the process

Expressions: Heaven forbid!
Whatever ya' say, boss.
Let's play Follow the Leader.
Forgive me, Father, for I have sinned.

Other Titles: The Pope; The High Priest; Master of the Mysteries of the Arcana

Key: Religion; teaching; the hermaphrodite; manifestation of knowledge; conscious; identity with the masses; psychic control; conscious earth teaching.

Combining man and God. The original idea of this archetype is the symbol of the male aspect of humanity that brings knowledge of the dualities within each person. The Hierophant represented physical teaching through active and conscious action—the Word brought forth onto the physical plane so that we could unite within by learning without. However, this idea has been lost in religion and society by the suppression of the feminine within and without, so that now the male side of consciousness usually dominates, resulting in the psychic control of identity with the masses and the loss of individuation. Before this split between the dualities, and for some few still, The Hierophant is the true religion obtained through right activity and right thought.

The Hierophant in a reading can mean either receiving or giving conscious earth teachings. This most often takes the form of an actual person, but it can also mean conscious teachings in any physical form, i.e., reading, writing, television. The Hierophant can also indicate right action—doing the right thing on the physical level.

—————————— VI · THE LOVERS ——————————

Golden Dawn Title: The Children of the Voice; The Oracle of the Mighty Gods

Astrological Sign: Gemini

Simple Letter: Smell

Phrase: Coming together

Expressions: Maybe—maybe not.
                     What on earth do I do now?
                     Will you please make up your mind?
                     He loves me—he loves me not—he loves me—he loves me not—he loves—

Other Titles: The Two Paths; Temptation; Love

Key: Choosing; spiritual harmony; identification; love; decision; to bind and join and to separate and divide; to have power to perceive and the power to act.

Spiritual harmony—the parallel development of the activity and susceptibility in us to know when to receive and when to act. To have power of perception plus the power of realization. Or to have neither, resulting in over-identification and confusion.

The Lovers card represents the myth of Cupid, which is why the card often depicts Cupid shooting an arrow down toward the three figures. Cupid is the young man in the center who, according to Jung, represents the self, or the χεῖδos behind ideas of unity and totality. The Mother, or older woman, is the self's shadow, usually depicted as a dark chthonic figure, because the shadow is the part of self that we have repressed into our subconscious. The younger woman is the self's anima (or animus for a woman), which the self is attempting to incorporate within self. Jung called the male and female joining together the "syzygy." Union of the pairs of opposites results in the self becoming whole and transcending consciousness.

When you receive the Lovers in a reading, you are, or will, go through a period of having to choose. There are usually two or more paths open to you. The Lovers can also mean over-identification and severe projections with another person, so that he or she is not perceived as he or she actually is, but as you would like the person to be. It is important when receiving The Lovers to keep the myth of Cupid in mind, because on some level in some way this is an issue. It does not always have to be a man-woman relationship issue, as the shadow (or mother) versus the syzygy in one's self is also an issue of resolving all those complexities within oneself that involve not recognizing the shadow and/or anima/animus, thus forcing these archetypal energies to be played out through others in our environment.

VII · THE CHARIOT

Golden Dawn Title: The Child of the Powers of the Waters; the Lord of the Triumph of Light

Astrological Sign: Cancer

Simple Letter: Speech

Phrase: Riding the wave

Expressions: Things are going my way.
You scratch my back and I'll scratch yours.
This is what I call living.
Just lucky, I guess.
All's well that ends well.

Other Titles: The Triumphal Car; Victory; The Chariot of Osiris

Key: Victory; foundation; everything in nature works toward the benefit of everything else if allowed to follow its own natural course.

How everything can be turned and used for one's own ends — seeing the bright side of everything. The proper law that each and every single thing can be used and improved upon for its and for one's own advantages. Knowing how to use something according to its own best nature and its own natural law. It is making the best of the situation, no matter how large or small. Like being an optimist because it works, because one believes in it; like planting a seed at its right phase of the Moon, in its most compatible soil, in the best location so it can flourish to its utmost. Knowing that for everything there is a season, a time for reaping, a time for sowing. It is believing that each and every thing works supremely to its own internal harmony if given the opportunity. It is saying, "I will do it this way because it is for its own best nature, thus it is also best for me." Sometimes it is landing on all fours after a free-fall — a solid foundation after a free-fall.

The Chariot in a reading usually signifies that things are going your way and will work out as you wish.

VIII · JUSTICE

Golden Dawn Title: The Daughter of the Lords of Truth; the Ruler of the Balance

Astrological Sign: Libra

Simple Letter: Work

Phrase: Taking the rap.

Expressions: Don't push your luck.
                 The worm turns.

I told you so.
I'm doing this for your own good.
Go ahead—make my day.

Other Titles: Adjustment; Themis; The Scales and the Blade

Key: Maintaining universal harmony and law; established balance; balance by opposites; action and reaction—the pendulum swings to its opposite; the law of karma.

The superconscious reminding the conscious of the subconscious. The word innocence derives from the word ignorant, or to ignore. To be innocent is the same thing as to be ignorant. And just as the Goddess Persephone was punished for her innocence, so does Justice punish us for our ignorance. It is not that we are punished for our sins, but rather we pay the price for ignoring. As the old cliche goes, "Ignorance is no excuse." Justice is not interested in punishing us for foolish ideas, morals, or ethics, she is interested in maintaining universal harmony and restoring the balance of spiritual law. She is concerned with preserving the universe as a whole.

Ignorance, like innocence, imagines that it is guiltless and blames other people for its own fate. Justice is the Major Arcanum that demonstrates the law of cause and effect—every action, thought, and desire comes back to us in equal magnitude, regardless of our ignorance in having been the original force that set it forth. Justice is the law of karma.

Justice received in a reading is like The Chariot in that harmony and balance are manifesting. However, the big difference is that with Justice sometimes its idea of harmony and balance is not the same as ours. It operates at a level that achieves balance in spite of what we may perceive or want that balance to be.

IX · THE HERMIT

Golden Dawn Title: The Prophet of the Eternal; the Magus of the Voice of Power

Astrological Sign: Virgo

Simple Letter: Sexual love

Phrase: Being yourself

Expressions: Bored, bored, bored.
Could you please move over just a little?
Why are you bothering me with this stuff?
Back off, Jack!
Not tonight, dear, I have a headache.
Oh, go paddle your own canoe!

Other Titles: Time; The Old Man; The Veiled Lamp; The Hunchback

Key: Self-initiation; Wise Old Man—meaning; being oneself; withdrawal; Time.

The Hermit is *time* because, just as time, he is "being" rather than "becoming." Time is what we use to measure our perceptions.

Time is things changing but staying the same;
things staying the same but changing.
Time is cycles within flow
and flow within cycles.
It is constant repetition within constant flow;
the eternal reoccurrence within eternal flow.
Time is a cycle, enfolding and unfolding,
in and out, exploding and imploding.
Time does not flow,
just as space does not flow.

It is we that flow,
wayfarers in a omnipresent Cosmos.

The Hermit symbolizes the need to live from your own values and not from someone else's. The need to go within and discover what it is you want rather than what it is you are supposed to want. The Hermit is an enigmatic card to receive in a reading because it involves being yourself, and it is seldom that you know yourself enough to be able to be yourself. All people have this problem.

When receiving The Hermit in a reading, look to yourself as best as possible to discover what it is *you* are and what it is *you* want in the situation, and not what it is you are supposed to be or want. Look to what pleases you and not to what pleases someone else. A period of withdrawal or solitude sometimes comes when you get The Hermit to entice you to better face yourself.

———— X · THE WHEEL OF FORTUNE ————

Golden Dawn Title: The Lord of the Forces of Life

Astrological Planet: Jupiter

Double Letter: Riches-Poverty

Phrase: Watching your destiny

Expressions: Next!
It's my turn.
Here we go again.
Play it again, Sam.
Tomorrow's another day.
What goes up, must come down.
You take the high road, and I'll take the low road.

Other Titles: Fortune; The Wheel; The Sphinx

Key: Destiny; fate; fortune; the instinctual forces that motivate the endless cycles of life; that which goes around comes around.

The natural cycle of the inner and outer. The Wheel of Fortune is the Mill of the Gods. The Mill of the Gods grinds slow and small and exceedingly well. It levels everything, raising one at the expense of the other, because all influences and their processes are reciprocal. Jung said that the way to the goal seems chaotic and interminable at first, and only gradually do the signs increase that it is leading anywhere. The way is straight but appears to go round in circles. More accurately, it goes in spirals around a defined center.

The average person is on the circumference of the Wheel, so that your own actions result in your reacting by going around from top to bottom, experiencing agony, ecstasy, boredom, confusion, over and over again. The enlightened person is anchored at the Wheel's hub, at your own center, so instead of being tossed around by your actions, you stand at the center of Higher Self, watching your destiny play out, knowing the way appears chaotic but is actually straight.

Many times when The Wheel card is received in a reading it indicates a new process has begun due to what you have set in motion from your past. This new unfoldment can be, and usually is, a rather long and ponderous process, manifesting itself in stages and evolving new paths rather than in immediate leaps and bounds. The Wheel indicates that something is happening or will happen as a natural result of what you have chosen.

XI · STRENGTH

Golden Dawn Title: The Daughter of the Flaming Sword

Astrological Sign: Leo

Simple Letter: Taste

Phrase: Trusting and allowing

Expressions: There's no reason to get all excited.
No problem.
Hey, hey, hey.
Big deal.
Don't worry about it.
What a pussycat!
Every dog may have his day, but the night belongs to us pussycats.

Other Titles: Fortitude; The Force; Lust; The Tamed Lion

Key: Instinct and/or Intuition; survival; instinctual compelling drive for protection or survival; winning; the hero; truest magic without attempting to direct the course of operation; understanding; compassion; fortitude; passive passion.

The instinctual nature (survival, lust, sex) is in harmony with the intuitive nature (love, understanding). This can be intuition at its keenest, or allowing instincts to act without restraint until they swallow us up. The instinctual nature thinks in terms of survival and will. When it is active, we tend to demand that our will be done the way we want it done and that our desires be satisfied. The intuitional nature thinks in terms of acceptance and faith. When intuition is active, we tend to accept that desires and goals will be satisfied according to The All's Will and that there is no difference between It's Will and our own. True prayer and magic is the leaving of the decision about the fulfillment of the request to The All.

When you receive Strength in a reading, it is time to trust and allow God to take care of things. Too many times Leo tries to do it alone, as it is sometimes easier to give (and control) than to receive (and not control). Strength means taking care of your inner and allowing and trusting The All to take care of the outer.

———————— XII · THE HANGED MAN ————————

Golden Dawn Title: The Spirit of the Mighty Waters

Astrological Planet: Neptune

Maternal Letter: Water-spiritual

Phrase: Obeying the spirit

Expressions: Hang in there.
You're wearing me out with this.
Whoops, I really blew that one!
Do you promise to tell the truth, the whole truth, and nothing but the truth?

Other Titles: The Traitor; The Drowned Man; The Sacrifice

Key: Salvation through obedience; completion; waiting for the right time; total surrender of self to higher power; losing.

Listening to and obeying your inner self even when it is opposed to what you think you need or want. It indicates a willingness to submit to the dictates of the inner self in spite of what seems logical or needed. It is guidance and wisdom from the unconscious that if not obeyed, results in suffering and defeat. This is the card of sacrifice. The Hanged Man is called the most purely spiritual card of the tarot—the Law of Sacrifice. Sacrifice means "to make sacred," to realize that there is no difference between our image of how things ought to be and how they really are.

The Hanged Man indicates loss of the ego, which is truly a sacrifice that makes sacred. It is in the loss of the personal ego that we come to understand that there is no difference between the words sacrifice and sacred. Initially, ego loss results in much suffering and confusion. After the loss of the ego there generally follows a period of knowing we have done away with the useless but are at a loss as to what to replace it with in this world. Our values are no longer the values of the masses, and we often don't know what to do with the new values. And people with little ego are forever variant from their fellow men, forever thereafter set apart from the crowd. But on most cards the Hanged Man has a smile on his face. It is a most enigmatic smile which only those who have sacrificed can share. It is the smile that knows the sacrifice will make sacred, and it is worth all the suffering and confusion that it brings.

The Hanged Man in a reading often indicates a time when your intellect or logic very clearly points you in one direction while your inner self or intuition just as clearly points you in the other. Your logic may tell you that if you follow the dictates of the obvious and don't rely on what appears to be concrete evidence, you are headed for disaster. But in the case of The Hanged Man, it will prove to be just the opposite. This is a time to accept, to surrender, and above all else, obey the Spirit.

XIII · DEATH

Golden Dawn Title: The Child of the Great Transformers; the Lord of the Gate of Death

Astrological Sign: Scorpio

Simple Letter: Movement

Phrase: Letting go

Expressions: Do I have to?
Catch ya' later?
You must have the wrong number.
Can't we talk about this?
Now?
Don't call me, I'll call you.
I can't right now — I have to wax the dog.

Other Titles: The Skeleton Reaper

Key: Total change; transformation; metamorphosis.

Every life consciousness has its own awareness. It is aware of its own domain in which it perceives with its own unique sensors while remaining unaware of other consciousnesses that live among it. A rock, a plant, a snail, an animal, a person—all remain largely unaware of another's world because of limited, but necessary, perceptions.

When we leave a certain perception we call it death. Because we can sense only what human beings can sense, when we leave human consciousness we say we have died, and we have turned from that consciousness, but we have not died. For, in truth, there is no death as we perceive it. There is really only unawareness of other consciousnesses.

When we die to this physical consciousness we are re-born to another. Death and birth are two words that are heavily laden with misconceptions. They should more appropriately be called movement, for in actuality, there is never any real death or birth, no real creation or destruction—everything is really just change, or motion.

When we lose perception of this physical plane, we gain perception of another. This is easier to see if we think about how we experience it every day of our lives. It is said that death is sleep because each night when we go to sleep we lose awareness of our physical plane, and each morning when we awaken we lose awareness of the plane where we slept. When an infant is born to parents on Earth, he has not really been born, he has merely become aware of Earth consciousness. That is why he is helpless at first, why we as adults must teach him Earth awareness. And when he grows old and dies to this plane, he gains awareness of another dimension.

God is already perfect, already Whole, and all of our parts, perceptions, separations, appearances of destruction and creation are but movements and cycles of our perceiving The One at particular angles.

We shall not cease from exploration
And the end of all our exploring

Will be to arrive where we started
And know the place for the first time.[3]

When you receive Death in a reading it is the end of your awareness of something. But there is no death without birth, and loss of perception means gaining a new perspective, a new awareness that replaces the old perception that you have now exchanged. Until we are whole, we continually exchange one angle for another, and the hope of all life is that we continually strive toward The Whole, gradually reaching the point where the gaining of a new angle also encompasses the retaining of the old. That is what wholeness means—never again experiencing separations because we now know that everything is merely one. We now stand in the center of the circle where we can see all rays instead of moving around the circumference perceiving only a few at a time.

XIV · TEMPERANCE

Golden Dawn Title: The Daughter of the Reconcilers; the Bringer Forth of Life

Astrological Sign: Sagittarius

Simple Letter: Anger

Phrase: Sharing with your angel

Expressions: Thank you.
It's been real.
Your place or mine?
Let's get together again sometime.
Thanks, I needed that.

Other Titles: Prudence; The Arrow; The Two Urns; Genius of the Sun

---

[3]T.S. Eliot, "Little Gidding of the Four Quartets," *The Complete Poems and Plays: 1909–1950* (New York: Harcourt Brace Jovanovich, 1952), p. 145.

Key: Guardian angel; moderation — not extreme nor excessive; blending of diverse elements; conjunction of the opposites.

Temperance often indicates that you are in the presence of your guardian angel, and she will help and advise you if you can listen. It is a combination of forces, the law of processes, in which you and your guardian angel, or inner guide, can achieve a balance and realization of what is available to both.

The best way to think of Temperance is in its literal sense. Temperance literally means (1) the mixing of opposite ingredients in proper proportion; and (2) care with the combination of elements. Your angel can guide you to mix with care the inner and outer elements, or show you how to best combine all ingredients in their proper proportions.

When you receive Temperance in a reading, it may be a good time to do meditation, such as creative visualization. It also means you are, or will, achieve a harmonious balance with the energies currently operating in your life. Sometimes Temperance can indicate so much harmony that stagnation results, but usually you will be aware of this because you have a feeling of boredom or apathy. This is why creative visualization is good either way because this form of meditation, if done correctly, usually encourages your outer life to change and grow. Receiving the Temperance card can also indicate opposite situations, or forces at work in your outer life that are delicately maintaining a fragile balance.

XV · THE DEVIL

Golden Dawn Title: The Lord of the Gates of Matter; the Child of the Forces of Time

Astrological Sign: Capricorn

Simple Letter: Mirth

Phrase: Butting in

Expressions: I never lie.

              I've seen it all.

              I've got it all.

              There's no place like me.

              It's all your fault!

              "Hallelujah, brother, the Lord has shown me the way to save your soul!" (Greater activation of the archetype can be achieved if one will thump a Bible while repeating this.)

Other Titles: Typhon

Key: Arrogance of the spirit; fragmentation; fear; boundaries and limitations.

Awareness is toward wholeness (whole-holy); unawareness is toward fragmentation or an unconscious egocentric use of power. This card symbolizes our own unconscious evil projected onto others as scapegoats who then appear to act against us on the outside. To be unaware of self is to create fragmentation rather than wholeness, for to be ignorant of the whole of good and evil within oneself is to divide ourself, projecting our unconscious onto others to placate and satisfy the inability to see ourself. It is rather like the sides of a box. What you see depends on which side of the box you are looking at.

Some theologians state that evil happens when we commit what we know to be a sin. In actuality, it is the opposite that is true. Only UNconsciousness can be evil. Consciousness cannot be evil, for it is only through what we do *not* know that we commit error. The card indicates arrogance of the spirit; truth without doubt; the belief that there is only one truth and that you are in possession of it. This seems to be the deepest root of all the evil that is in the world.

The Devil can mean many things in a reading, depending on what the Devil is to us. It most often indicates fear in some form because we fear what we don't understand. When we receive The Devil in a reading, we need to watch for possible arrogance, fear, or placing self-imposed limitations on ourselves. Sometimes there is someone or something in the environment onto whom we are placing negative projections of evil or wrong.

XVI · THE TOWER

Golden Dawn Title: The Lord of the Hosts of the Mighty

Astrological Planet: Mars

Double Letter: Grace-indignation

Phrase: Getting off the fence

Expressions: Dear John,
You can't be serious!
Holy Cow!
Is there a doctor in the house?
Life is just full of little surprises.
Here I come, ready or not!

Other Titles: The House of God; The Lightning-Struck Tower; Fire From Heaven

Key: Sudden truth or flash of enlightenment; changing a basic or core belief; Tower of Babel — the mouth.

This card indicates a connection that is in a state of tension, a connection that results in the affirmation of one and the exclusion of the other. A sudden bolt, which causes you to focus intensely on one issue in order to receive clarity.

The card can bring a state of grace. Sometimes a Tower event can bring an accident or damage which, if you react with indignation, will result in loss. However, if you respond with trust or acceptance, a Tower event can bring grace like you wouldn't believe!

When you get The Tower in a reading, prepare for a sudden happening or event to occur in your life. Like lightning, it will either be awesome and spectacular, or shattering and damaging. Either way it will change how you previously felt or what you previously believed about something or someone.

XVII · THE STAR

Golden Dawn Title: The Daughters of the Firmament; the Dweller between the Waters

Astrological Sign: Aquarius

Simple Letter: Imagination

Phrase: Gaining an inner view

Expressions: I can't believe I ate the whole thing.
What a view.
Far out.
Yum.
May the Force be with you.
Thank your lucky stars.

Other Titles: The Stars; The Tower of the Magi

Key: Receiving help from above; natural divination; a new flow of energy and resources; unexpected help; hopes and wishes come true; uniting inner and outer in reality.

Inspiration, clarity of vision, insight and understanding bringing creativity and unexpected help. The two impulses of life—to "live" life and to "know" life—in harmony. Uniting all experience, inner and outer, to create a new reality. Higher Self in harmony with lower self.

There is an old qabalistic saying to the effect of, "When you find the beginning of the way—the star of your soul will show its light." Joseph Campbell said that life should be "following your bliss," and that when you find and follow your path, invisible hands reach out to help you. All the universe comes to your aid, and doors open as if by magic. Or as Jonathan Livingston

Seagull so wisely uttered, "When it is right, nothing can stop it. When it is wrong, nothing can make it happen." This is why The Star sometimes shows a woman reaching from the heavens with one hand and toward the Earth with the other because this arcanum is receiving help from above to manifest below. You are following the path of your heart, thus flowing with universal harmony.

When you receive The Star in a reading, it is often like blessings flowing from above and grounding themselves into your life. It brings a feeling of contentment and abundance, as if your faith is based on fact and not on hope. It brings the enjoyment of both the rose and its thorns, the inner peace and knowledge of, "What difference does it make? All is going according to plan."

XVIII · THE MOON

Golden Dawn Title: The Ruler of the Flux and Reflux; the Child of the Sons of the Mighty

Astrological Sign: Pisces

Simple Letter: Sleep

Phrase: Giving up

Expressions: Now where did I put those keys?
Is this mid-life crisis?
Are we having fun yet?
He's out to lunch.
The lights are on, but no one's home.
I think he has a hole in his screen door.
I think the cheese has fallen off his cracker.
Yoo, hoo, is anybody there?

Other Titles: The Twilight

Key: The Dark Night of the Soul; mechanicalness; hidden from the conscious.

Because The Moon is hidden from the conscious, one can only wait and see. One is unable to move forward—unable to go back. There is no help from the intellect or from "old ways," no turning back. One can only move forward with an understanding heart knowing that help will come *only* from the unknown.

One difference between The Hanged Man and The Moon is that with The Hanged Man the intellect beckons and tempts. With The Moon, the intellect is gone and doesn't even entice.

The card represents diffuse awareness—no ability to reach focused consciousness. The unconscious, with its diffuse awareness, must be relied upon. The Moon is that which is hidden and defuse, intuition and feeling, and in that sense, all that is esoteric. It is the invisible and the unreal in the sense of being non-physical. The dark half of yin-yang.

When you get The Moon in a reading there is nothing you can do. It is out of your hands. Forget it. No amount of thinking or worrying or planning is going to help. Things are happening on an inner level now and you can neither see nor hear them, and there is nothing to do but to go about your business elsewhere, if you can, for the time being.

XIX · THE SUN

Golden Dawn Title: The Lord of the Fire of the World

Astrological Planet: Sun

Double Letter: Fertile-barren

Phrase: Seeing the light

Expressions: Life is just a bowl of cherries.
I want it NOW!
Happy days are here again.
Great balls of fire!
Where are my shades?

Other Titles: The Blazing Light

Key: Manifestation; good time; child-wholeness; futurity; the bringer of light.

This card represents the power of the rise of the unconscious to the conscious. It indicates the experience of being aware of the archetype heaving itself from within to consciousness—its cataclysmic upheaval and take-over. It is the rightness of the universe, focused consciousness, that which is present, substantial, obvious, real, the physical, the sum of thinking and sensation, and in that sense, all that is exoteric. It is the ability of focused consciousness to identify and to act. The Sun is the complement of The Moon because The Moon is female diffuse awareness and The Sun is male focused consciousness. The light half of yin-yang.

Jung said that the Child Archetype is nearly always a condition of futurity. Due to a coming together on the inner at the present, The Sun is an event or situation that will manifest in the future.

When you receive The Sun in a reading, it means that something was once fragmented and now has become whole. It indicates that the astral forces have accomplished this on the inner, and that this new wholeness is now hurdling its way to the outer, or to your physical world.

XX · JUDGEMENT

Golden Dawn Title: The spirit of the Primal Fire

Astrological Planet: Pluto

Maternal Letter: Fire-spiritual

Phrase: Beginning again

Expressions: Wow, *déjà vu!*
It's been a while.
If I'd known you were coming I'd have baked a cake.

Where have you been all my life?
They're never going to believe this back home.

Other Titles: The Angel; The Last Judgement; The Aeon; The Awakening of the Dead; Genius of the Dead

Key: Ending the old and beginning the new; astral transformation; rewards and summation of past efforts; arrival of the future that we have created from the past; reaping what has been sown.

Judgement is the re-birth of Birth after the re-death of Death. This is the creation that follows the sound of the Word. It is changes in time caused by divine attraction, so that divine nature is manifest. Judgement is called the archetype of divine attraction because we must be reborn into what we *are* by virtue of like *always* attracting like. It expresses changes in time because often we get what we want only *after* we don't consciously want it anymore. The astral vortexes of love and desire can only manifest on the physical plane after they have been consciously released by the mind. As long as we still actively hold on to them in thought or emotion they cannot leave to express physically. We are actually holding on to them and preventing their happening because physical energy can only be in one place at a time. Likewise, when we hold on to physical energy, we prevent it from being released into its spiritual form.

When you receive Judgement in a reading, you are going on to another aspect of yourself. It signifies the arrival of the future that you have created from your past. You will experience not what you consciously think you need or want, but only what you unconsciously are.

───── XXI · THE WORLD ─────

Golden Dawn Title: The Great One of the Night of Time

Astrological Planet: Saturn

Double Letter: Power-servitude

Phrase: Understanding the reason for your being

Expressions: I'm outta here.
That's the whole ball of wax.
To be or not to be, that is the question.
On a clear day you can see forever.
I finally got it all together and remember where I put it.

Other Titles: The Universe; The Crown of the Magi

Key: Discovering your purpose in life; living life to its greatest possible abundance—to the fullness of your being.

The World signifies people who cannot be defeated because they are not fighting anything. They do not want anything that is in opposition to universal law. In discovering their own true desires, and living them, they receive the support of the Universe. The World symbolizes not being afraid, being comfortable with themselves, and loving the world.

It is difficult for many of us to know what our purpose in life is. "What is the meaning of my life?" has been the question that has haunted people ever since we first became aware enough to ask it, and we have been asking it ever since. Each of us possess the ability and has the right to express in our own unique and creative way, whether by making pottery, studying zoology, flying kites, or making corporate decisions. To live to the fullness of our being means both to *know* and to be able to *do* what we love. If we discover what we love and then do it, we are working in accordance with universal law. We cannot do otherwise for activity done in love is the ultimate expression of God.

Some of us know what we want but find ourselves unable to have it because of our life's circumstances. To possess The World we must have both the knowledge of what we want *and* the courage to do it. It is seldom, if ever, easy. The World is the last Arcanum, at the end of all the others, because it is the goal reached at the end of the struggle. It is the last and greatest goal because it *is* us. It is discovering our purpose. It brings us joy and bliss, for when we find and live our own individual purpose we are fulfilling the reason for being.

People who understand the symbolism of The World are endowed with both power and the desire to serve. Don Juan told Carlos Castanada that power is the ability to manifest intentions. Power means power *in*, not power *over*. When we use power in accordance with universal law, we are not separate and alone in the Universe; we are, in reality, part of the Universe, and in understanding that we see why we can never have power over anything.

When you receive The World in a reading, look for clues that will help you discover the reason for your being. The World card is telling you that your purpose is very close or very far from you, but either way, your purpose in life is the issue right now.

Special Insights

As in the Minor Arcana, with its "dark" cards, there are a few cards in the Major Arcana that need further explanation, either to clear up misconceptions or to clarify what they mean in a reading. In dealing with them separately here, I hope to give students of tarot a better understanding of these cards, a deeper layer of meaning than the previous summary of their characteristics. Armed with further insight, students can then proceed with the readings that follow.

I · THE MAGUS

The Magus (or the Magician) shares several intrinsic qualities with the High Priestess, the Hierophant, and Strength. When dealing with any of these four archetypes it is easy enough to confuse them because even though their differences are evident, their similarities are not so clear, and when reading descriptions of them we can get the feeling that we have definitely missed something in the translation. It may be somewhat ambiguous to address similarities among the four because all are so vague, binary, subtle, and magical that definite distinctions often break down. But, hopefully, the Magus, being the congenial merrymaker he is, can see a little humor in the illusion of this.

Some books say that the Magus is the masculine counterpart to the feminine High Priestess—the Magus being yang energy while the High Priestess is yin. While the Magus is indeed yang, and the High Priestess yin, the two cards are not counterparts to one another. They are two separate distinctive archetypes with very differing motions, forms, and purposes. What the two cards *do* have in common, however, is that both the Magus and the High Priestess bring energy forth from the pure unformed archetypal world into the worlds below in the form of magic. The Magus usually brings it with aggressive, focused consciousness, so much so that it is frequently seen to break into the physical plane in such forms as answers to prayers, wish fulfillment, bad luck, good luck, strokes of fate, synchronicities and coincidences. The High Priestess brings energy from the pure archetypal world into the lower planes with passivity and diffuse awareness. She requires intense veneration if you want to see her and deep quietitude to hear her. The Magus is sometimes seen when archetypal messages erupt into physical manifestation or consciousness, while the High Priestess is more inner plane, as she is recognized in dreams, hunches, impulses, feelings, or in meditation. It is simplistic to say that the Magus is focused, and the High Priestess is diffused, but it does help us distinguish between the two.

Some say that the Magus is the masculine counterpart to the feminine High Priestess, while others say her partner is the Hierophant. The comparison of the latter two is much closer to the truth, which is why in earlier times the two cards were called the High Priest and the High Priestess, and the Pope and the Popess. Both cards are symbols of spiritual messages being brought forth through a physical medium. While the High Priestess brings her messages to us *indirectly* through the subconscious or through the shadows of our deepest dreams, the Hierophant brings his messages *directly* to our conscious minds as he preaches to us from his pulpit. These two cards are truly the yin and yang of spiritual teaching—the High Priestess being indirect, emotional, feminine, diffuse awareness and the Hierophant being direct, physical, masculine, focused consciousness.

What does the Magus have in common with these two teaching arcana? This is where, once again, the Magus displays his magic show. He is Mercury, the androgenous one, the archetype that combines both the High Priestess and the Hierophant in his ability to reach us on both planes. He can reach us directly *and* indirectly, both through our dreams and through our everyday lives—whichever is most convenient for his purpose and time. He is very much the ruler of synchronicity—the unconsciousness of the High Priestess erupting into the consciousness of the Hierophant.

The Magus is also similar to both the Hierophant and Strength in that all three can involve matters of magic that reach our attention and possible participation. The Hierophant can involve active magic, such as ritual and mantras, the invocation being directed from us to our desired goal. The Hierophant's number is five, the number given to human beings. This is why five is the number used in most magical rituals, amulets, and talismans, because it is the number of magic used to obtain human desires. The five-sided pentagram is famous for its use in magic ritual and seeking the bidding of wish fulfillment.

Originally the Hierophant's message was that human beings are to be co-workers with The All, but this original message has been misinterpreted, so that now the number five and the Hierophant all too often mean the church as God, the Pope as God, Jesus as God, man as God—just about anything as God except God. The Hierophant has come to mean using mantra and prayer to achieve the personal ends of the church, or to achieve physical desires. We have forgotten that people are only part of the program—not the entire program—and that God is *all* life everywhere.

Strength, as compared to the active magic of the Hierophant, is usually seen as more passive magic, sometimes involving ritual and mantras, the difference being that the course of operation is not directed. The direction is not seen as from the source to another specific source in a defined way, but rather from the source as the source sees best, trusting God to know what is required for all concerned.

And once again, the Magus displays his magic and mastery of illusion by combining both the active magic of the Hierophant and the passive magic of Strength. To the Magus goes the achievement of both, a perfect balance of magic performed from the Gods, for he can either bring the physical requests of the Hierophant in the passive mode of Strength, or bring the passive magic of Strength with the concrete direct results of the Hierophant, but always successfully giving us our desires in accordance with exact price extracted as was originally decreed by the Gods.

In all four cards the key word is *love.* In any magical action, love must overwhelm and infuse, or foolishness and danger can result. To attempt any form of magic without love being involved in the symmetries of the magician, the ritual, and the goal is to invite the option of *anything.* Since it is difficult to judge whether love is present in ourselves, our motivation, and the object or subject of the magic ritual, it is advisable to summon the Magus *only* by leaving all things under the will of God. It is easy to deceive ourselves into believing we are being motivated by love, when sometimes our true motivation is more often desire. Like will always attract like, and to summon the Magus is to summon exactly what we are, no more and no less. But it is an excellent way to find out just exactly what it is we indeed are, if we are prepared for surprises and shocks.

The Magus works his magic with or without conscious acknowledgement. He is part of universal law and does not deliver his messages for the personality, but for the Gods. He does not come to deliver a moral lesson or message to our egos, but rather is part of the Whole in its natural function. He is not concerned with who we think or believe ourselves to be, for he knows it is more often the case that we are not at all who we believe ourselves to be. It's easy to see, under the circumstances, why he finds such humor and duality in our requests.

The Magus also performs his magic through synchronicities. Synchronicities and coincidences – the messages of the Gods – delivered via the Magus, are all around us. They are not only in the car, but also in family, friends, work, pets, home, garden, ashtray, telephone, vacuum sweeper, and coffee pot – in all those people and things around us with whom we have formed inter-related symmetries. Their rhythms mingle with our own so that when one is altered, all matrices oscillating in the same force field are adjusted and effected accordingly. Distance and locality are of little consequence because the Magus knows not time nor space.

It may be that we cannot influence others with conscious intentions, but the unconscious is a horse of a different color. The unconscious is the abode of the archetypes – the all-powerful Gods – and they deliver the messages of their presence and power in our lives by the Magus. By recognizing the many messages, we can see that what we are in the unconscious is also what we have in the conscious environment around us. Whether the Magus is summoned by conscious or unconscious magic, it is through the unconscious that he comes. The unconscious is his playground, and he is active in all of life by its and his very nature. He seems like magic to us because he notifies the known conscious physical world of what is already existing in our unknown unconscious psyche.

The Magus, the High Priestess, the Hierophant, and Strength all play their respective parts in the magic of our lives, each according to its own archetypal resonance. They and we together, along with all forms of consciousness, play our parts in the magical dance of life, intertwining all our realities in an intricate infinitude of dynamic creation and destruction.

III · THE EMPRESS

All the Universe as we know it is held together by what the Empress represents. She is motion by allurement, love, gravity, the glue of all things that have consciousness.

The planets circle each other in their endless dance of allurement, clinging to one another in their orbits, reaching and holding on to one another through the force of their mutual attractions. The stars are born and the stars explode, sending their billions of star embryos into space, eventually to be formed once again out of themselves or to be drawn through allurement to another plane that beckons.

All of consciousness seeks what it knows, for to know is to become aware, and to become aware is to love. It is how all of life creates itself out of itself, because life loves what it is aware of, and through its awareness of itself, it creates more of itself. Sometimes human beings have problems with love. From our first awareness of love, and even before, we struggle to come to terms with the concept. From the womb of the Empress who bears us to the arms of Death who takes us, we struggle to become aware, to love. We run from love in ignorance, we deny it with hate. We kill it from fear, and we wound it with doubt. But in the end, we cannot deny the Empress, for she will not leave us. She remains—waiting, hoping, loving. She watches us; she grieves for our attention, knowing that if we can but turn our eyes to her, we will be overcome with joy. Love has as many definitions as it does forms. One cannot define its essence – only know it. All else is description of effect.

If you are not sure you are loved by the Gods and Goddesses, all you need do is to be very still, look around, and see yourself and all the majesty of the Universe held together with love's force. Love is all around us in all that is, for the Universe is the All-That-Is.

All things come into themselves and out of themselves, propelled by one force and one force only – love. In it we find ourselves. If we can but love, the Empress will laugh and dance, and the Gods will weep with gratitude, for our joy is their joy, and their joy is our joy. The Empress asks only that we love, for there is no greater purpose, no other greater experience.

The All in its love for Itself created consciousness. Life is God living Itself. life is God learning Itself. Life is God loving Itself.

———————— V · THE HIEROPHANT ————————

Who is there among us who doesn't sometimes (many times, nearly all the time?) forget to practice what we preach? Actually, it's not so much a matter of forgetting to practice what we preach as it is a matter of not knowing that we aren't practicing what we preach. That may sound strange, but it happens all the time, even to those of us who think we are trying the hardest.

Have reverence for the Hierophant, for the Hierophant is trying to speak to us of the truth, and we cannot hear him. Think of how tiresome this job is. He is the hermaphrodite who is the keeper of dualities. His is not the plane of the Magician who delivers the message and then splits. He has the thankless job of sticking around to interpret the message that he delivers. The knowledge he knows in his wholeness he must translate into its parts. What he possesses as a whole he must witness being desecrated into fragments. His is the job of "doing the best he can under the circumstances," and the circumstances are not all that great. Of all the Arcana, The Hierophant is the one who reminds us of the axiom, "The answer can never be given—it can only be received."

He stands and delivers his message in its completeness and in its perfection, and we sit and receive his message in its parts and in its imperfection. The Hierophant says, "*See* this," and we say, "Okay, I see this." The Hierophant says, "Look again," and we say, "Yeah, I got it." The Hierophant sighs, for he knows that we have not gotten it, but have mutilated and torn it into a thousand little pieces according to our own thousand separate beliefs.

But still the Hierophant perseveres. He is steady and stable, willing and able. He keeps at us, knowing that someday something will occur to us in spite of ourselves. One could say that with some he has given up, and says, "Oh well, you haven't gotten it, so do the best you can do by just following the rules. At least right activity is better than nothing." On the other hand, it may be that he *is* right activity. Certainly, he is the dispenser of knowledge on the physical plane.

There are two aspects to the Hierophant. One is when he is someone else in your life who is a teacher. When he is another person who is a wise teacher, you can learn from his wisdom. The other aspect of the Hierophant is when he is yourself, existing in each of us, and you are dispensers of knowledge. What does this mean? Each of you is here for a reason—a very personal reason—and it is the Hierophant who reminds you that you are here to live your own individual purpose. If you do not eventually manifest onto the physical plane what you have become and know in your mind, in your emotions, and in your spirit, what growth can your personal purpose bring to us? If you do not recognize that all steps of the process are necessary, including manifesting and bringing forth your knowledge, then for what have you come into physical form, if not for manifestation?

If you have reached the point where a portion of your energy is sacred (sacred meaning to sacrifice), or perfected, and the point where that energy is to be utilized to its best advantage for your own personal growth and for the growth of The Whole, what will it profit you if you do not ground your knowledge and sacred energy onto the Earth in your actions and way of life? You will be giving little bits of yourselves away like hamburger. Giving a piece there, a piece here, wherever you happen to have fun putting it or feel the desire to expend it. But there is a point in all stages of evolvement where that energy is to go from perfection to completion, from the inner to the outer, from knowing to doing. It is to be put forth in the correct manner—scattered, yes, but scattered in knowledge and serving—not in ignorance and waste.

The Hierophant does this and reminds you that you are to do this. He is telling you to be the energy of the 5 that comes after the completion of the 4. He is that in you that tells you not to stop now for your job is not yet completed.

This is no simple job for us either. How much easier it is to maintain in the spirit what we believe to be whole instead of seeing it disillusioned and violated when we bring it to the physical. For surely it will be. It cannot be otherwise.

To keep it inside is to believe it pure. To put it outside is for the first time to know it as impure. But it is only through its impurity that true purity can be obtained. Until then it remains a glass of the finest wine that has not been tasted, or the fleetest of stallions that has not yet run. Just as the wine decreases in its glass after being tasted, and the stallion's legs are tried from his run, so will our energy be drained when it is expressed. But so it must be, for this is the world of duality, and in order to reach wholeness we must experience it in its parts, in its illusion, and in its struggle.

We cannot cast our pearls before swine without expecting them to be trampled. For trampled they most surely will be. The Hierophant can tell us all about that. He's an expect on the subject. But what do we do without him? What if he did not cast his pearls before us for us to trample? How then would one of us know of a single pearl, and how would the Hierophant manifest his perfection?

This does not mean that we are to go out and preach to others for them to be what we are, or that others are supposed to believe what we believe. This is the opposite of what the Hierophant intends, and why he is saddened to see that is what people have done with his teachings. This is not practicing what we preach.

He intends for each of us to *do* and to *be* what we preach—to have the courage and the strength to *be* ourselves and to *live* ourselves. To have the perfection of being what we are and not the imperfection of telling others to be for us what we cannot be for ourselves.

The Hierophant means to have the wisdom and commitment to go out and scatter our pearls, to do what we love to do, to love whom we want or need to love, to pursue the path our heart calls us to, knowing full well that we may be despised, misunderstood, or rejected, but do it anyway. It means having the commitment to love even if it means sacrifice, even if it means pollution. For to bind oneself to another person is to become part of his aura, part of his virtue, as well as part of his pollution. It means casting our pearls before swine because how can we do less than what the Hierophant does? The Hierophant is in us. He demands expression for he is expression. He is expression of the WORD, the LOGOS, that part of each of us that is our chosen path, our reason for returning.

The Hierophant is *knowledge made manifest*. How very contradictory these two principals are—knowledge and manifestation. In their very essences they are adversaries. Knowledge can maintain the illusion of purity, manifestation cannot.

We must be willing to become impure in order to become truely pure. We must lose it in order to gain it. Only then will we know what true purity is. For knowledge can be perfect, but it is not complete. To be perfect is not to be complete. To be complete is not to be perfect. Only through the Hierophant can we learn that true purity is both knowing *and* doing, both perfection *and* completion.

When we have reached the 4 we must go on to brave the 5. The Hierophant is telling us about both. He is saying "Risk it," for in the end we must anyway. In the end, if not in this lifetime, then another, we must eventually practice what we preach.

XII · THE HANGED MAN

Sometimes I'm inclined to believe all of life's problems can be broken down to only a few basic issues. Other times, I think that it must be infinitely more complicated than that. Assuming the former, I'm becoming convinced that one basic issue must have something to do with control. It is the Hanged Man who represents what this control issue is all about, and maybe he is having the same problem with control as we are because on some cards he is smiling and on some he is crying. On some cards he is holding a bag of gold, while on others his hands are tied behind his back. Most cards interpret him as hanging, but there are some that show him standing. By the gleeful sorrow represented in the card, we wonder whether the Hanged Man is being punished or rewarded. If this is reward, it doesn't appear all that great. On the other hand, his smile seems to indicate he may think it is. When studying the card, we are left with the distinct impression that the Hanged Man knows something we don't — a great big something.

How much of what we do and strive to be or to obtain in life is dominated by an unconscious need to control? Control is a nasty word to the esoteric mind, so we tend to say, "Oooh, not me! I don't know anything about that. I'm not interested in that nasty word." But in reality we must be terribly interested. For whether we are aware of it or not, each and every one of our lives is inundated with our blatent lack of control. We don't like to think that's true, and most certainly, you won't find many of us dwelling on that issue for too long, if at all. After all, lack of control is something that applies to the other guy, not us. And for some, especially the young, they are not yet aware that control is not possible. It is only when life suddenly hits us upside the head with the very real fact that we don't control that we are then kind of forced to go to pieces.

What is there exactly that we do control? What is it that we *can* control? How frightening it is to realize in the innermost depth of our being that we are out of control of just about everything in our life—that which will happen to us, around us, and to those we love or need most.

Consciously, we do not control our birth. We do not control our death. And the premise is that we control precious little of anything that goes in between. We've created a nice fat complacent society that does everything in its power to make us believe and behave differently, but the simple fact is, "Forget it."

We are at the mercy of the greater Forces of life. It is quite comforting to say, "The Lord is benevolent, and he'll take care of me." But the fact is we have no idea of what The Lord's definition of taking care of us means. We can certainly portend to know, as a great many do, and ease our nagging fears and aching minds with our faith in a protecting Father (Whatever happened to Mom?), but if we have the presence of mind to look at things the way they really are, we have to ask ourselves whether God's definition of a good time is always the same as our own!

It is equally comforting to say, "I don't smoke, I don't do drugs, and I drive carefully, so I'll have a nice long healthy life." The reality is we haven't the slightest idea what disease is lurking around the corner to snap its angry jaws at us, or where we will be on the day some other guy chooses to run a red light or stop sign. We don't know if on some seemingly normal average day we will find ourselves at the right place at the wrong time, or at the wrong place at the right time.

The reality is that non-smokers die of lung cancer, too; people who don't exercise live just as long as those who do; health addicts, athletes, joggers, vegetarians, preachers, teachers, mystics, priests, monks, and lamas die at no younger and no older age than the rest of us, and it is certain they suffer both mental and physical pain along the way, just like everyone else.

We can say all we want, "She's my best friend, and she'll never quit being here for me," or "He's my child, and he'll always love me." However, life can, and does, show us differently. There are just as many undevoted children as there are devoted children, a friend of twenty years can suddenly be "too busy" for our companionship, and divorces (whose origination began with "till death do us part") are as commonplace as the "till death do us part" ceremonies that began them. It would appear that we cannot speak for another person, no matter how well-loved or needed that person may be, nor can we begin to fathom what our own personal realities will bring us in the process of living.

There is the occult, or psychological, belief that if we change or become aware of ourselves that our environment and life will change accordingly. Certainly, this is valid. We might even begin to get the idea that a little bit of self-awareness will bring us a gift in the form of a little personal control. Certainly there are a great many books and teachers around these days telling us this is so. However, in what manner may we judge just how it is that we have accepted, grown, or changed our awareness in order to ascertain any degree of control? For we know not what doors we have opened in the closing of doors behind us, or what lies beyond doors yet unopened. And if we have *truly* obtained a degree of awareness, then we know for sure we can be the Hanged Man, for in increasing our awareness we have opened up ourselves to the possibilities of all of life and to the Will of the Whole. Awareness brings with it the desire for the good of The All, in which Its Will is the desire, not always our own. This is not to imply that our desire and the desire of God may not be synonymous, for indeed they may be and often are. But as human beings we cannot know anything other than what our limited spiritual and physical senses bring to us, and when considered in the light of the infinite, it is like saying a single flea has control over the dog.

Esoterically speaking, we can hope that all is being worked according to plan, and that in the general overall scheme of things, things will work out best for us if we live the best we are able according to our own code of honor. And this is probably true. At least, there is that belief, or hope, or promise. This doesn't do a whole heck of a lot, however, for our present lifetime, when we are struggling with forces unknown from within and without. To say that we have control over our personal life because of the Greater Plan is, by necessity, to have to re-define control—God's or ours.

That is the Hanged Man. No matter how we consciously attempt to control, the unconscious *knows* that the control can be taken from our hands at any moment. The Hanged Man is losing. The Hanged Man is everyone's possibility, Achille's heel, stroke of fate, likelihood.

How fragile we remain as human beings! If it is true (as the Buddhists believe) that we choose our destinies before entering the Earth plane by our propensity of character, that still gives little comfort to the conscious mind, for it can't remember what the destiny is that it chose while being unconscious. Many people believe with all their hearts that they do actually control their lives. Their error is usually they believe they consciously control their lives, never realizing that conscious control is but an illusion, until suddenly one day life shows them differently. What the *un*conscious is up to—where personal control really lays—is quite beyond their ability to know. For if they knew, then it would not be *un*conscious.

On some cards the Hanged Man is smiling. Maybe that is because he knows something we don't. In the final analysis we cannot control. In the final analysis that is faith. We struggle to control, we struggle to survive, we struggle and struggle and struggle, and yet for all our struggling, the Hanged Man is our final destination. We don't know for sure what it is that he knows. But maybe, just maybe, his smile is telling us that once we have truly acknowledged our lack of control we will suddenly discover that it was all for nothing. The illusion of control was only that—illusion—and we will go from believing we can control to knowing that for all our struggling, in the end there never was really anything at all for us to control.

Faith is not belief based upon fear of not believing. Faith is not acceptance of a doctrine because of laziness or lack of desire to question that doctrine. Faith is not acceptance of what we've always known or been taught because it has worked pretty good so far. Faith is trust based on knowledge. And only after knowledge has been gained, can faith then take over. There can be no faith without knowledge, for faith requires as its foundation, knowledge. Before that it is merely credulity. True faith is knowing that any human control is ultimately illusion, and knowing that regardless of what occurs to our personal worlds and realities that God is the only one that has got the program under control.

Perhaps the Hanged Man has learned, or is learning, that total surrender to the Spirit means relinquishing control to God who knows the program because It wrote it, directed it, and produced it. If the Hanged Man's part in the production isn't exactly what he had in mind, he still smiles for he *knows* that the control is in the right hands and all is going according to plan. He knows this because his faith is based on knowledge, or if it's not, it soon will be.

The Hanged Man may be learning but one lesson out of a myriad of intricate teachings, but my hunch is that this control issue is a basic. My hunch is that in truly relinquishing control, or relinquishing our fear of not possessing it, that we enter the realm of Arcanum XXI, the World, where faith is trust without reservation, where the final knowledge is knowing that we cannot know, and where we finally realize that there is no difference between our image of how things ought to be and how they really are.

XIII · Death and XX · Judgement

Students may at first be intimidated when encountering the Death or Judgement cards in a reading. We must realize that these cards represent change and transition, for they are a natural part of our human cycle and not to be feared. In explaining their occurrence in a layout, a reader may want to consider some of the following thoughts.

There is no death, and there is no birth. There is only re-death and re-birth, constantly being re-dead and re-born in a cycle perpetuated by the fires, waters, airs, and earths of desire. We are what we love, we become aware of what we love, are becoming what we love. Love is awareness. We go to what we are aware of—to what we love—over and over again, never ending, never beginning, always ending and beginning.

There is with death the pain of leaving behind what we love. The pain is all, it is overwhelming, and it screams from the totality of what we are, pain without equal. It screams out from our primal soul in its agony of leaving what and who we love. No! No! No! It reaches back with arms of agony—don't take me from that I love! NO!

The pain is in the soul of being, and there is that brief moment when the pain is so deep and total that there is *Death*. The pain is experienced in the fires of our spirits, in the waters of our souls, in the airs of our minds, and in the earths of our physical body. The pain of leaving our love behind clutches at our entire being. We fight and cling and reach out not to leave behind us all that we love. The pain is physical. We are immersed in gripping agony of the whole body, we clutch the stomach, double over, and we scream more and more. It cannot be. It is at the moment of dying that we know, truly know, without a veil, that we love with all our being.

Then comes re-birth. Still the spirit burns, the mind fights, the soul aches, and the body hurts. We hold our stomach and moan. All is lost. The pain cannot be borne. Then we are someplace else. The transition has been made. In the process of dying we blinked on and off, then we blinked in completely, into our new world of re-birth. We are too miserable, too full of pain to look around us.

But then someone reaches out to us. There are faces, and arms reaching out to us, trying to touch us, but we cannot see them. Gradually, so slowly at first, the physical pain gripping us still, and our hearts broken from death still, gradually, we open our eyes.

And there around us are the faces of those we have loved once before, so very very long ago, even before those we have just left in death. In front of us there is the face of the one we loved so very much most of all, a face that we also left once before in the same way of death, a face that at one time we thought we would never stop grieving and longing for. A face that we loved lifetimes ago that the mind misplaced, but the heart treasured. This one reaches out for us with his warmth and says, "I know. I know. I love you now, and always, and it will be okay."

There is a time during this transition, from the very first pale blinkings of dying through the intense blinking, to the time of complete transition and a time beyond, when both loves are held in the soul and memory. We pine and grieve for that which we have left, and we sigh with gratitude and acceptance when returning to others that we loved prior to those we just left.

Then, with what appears to be time, our awareness of our most recent lost love and of the past fades, for it is replaced with new memories of being with new, yet ever ancient, love that has awaited us. And yet there remains lingering an unfillable and unquenchable emptiness that eventually becomes undefinable.

And we cry, and we look at the world with fresh eyes that are ever wiser and kinder. Our tears are tears of gaining and losing, of going and coming, leaving behind and coming together. And with even greater time, the pain of leaving behind also dies, and we are, once again, only with those we love.

We look around us. Re-death and re-birth are everywhere. There is only never-ending ceaseless cycles. The flowers bloom and die, the Winter brings re-death, and the Spring re-birth. We see for the first time that all that exists dies and is born, forever and ever.

Is it, when we finally become totally aware, that we need never leave that which we have loved, and that all that we have become aware of, we become, that always it is with us?

CHAPTER 12

Reading the Cards

In this chapter we are going to think about reading the cards, laying them out, how to treat them in a reading, etc. The specific layouts follow.

The first thing to do when beginning a reading is to locate the card that will be used as the significator of the reading. The significator is always a court card and it represents the person you are reading for. This means that when you are doing readings for yourself, most of the time your significator will be the same card. The court card that most represents you is the one that symbolizes your superior function. Sometimes you may feel more like your auxiliary function, in which case you will feel like choosing the court card that represents that part of yourself. By and large, however, you will probably be more comfortable choosing the court card that is your superior function. Since most of you do not have the opportunity to take the Myers-Briggs Type Indicator to ascertain your personality type,[1] the next best thing is to go with your Intuition. Sometimes your Intuition picks out its correct court card because the conscious and unconscious are drawn to the appropriate card by the harmonizing attraction of like recognition. For obvious reasons, though, this method is not to be relied on if absolute verified accuracy is desired.

---

[1]See chapter 9, "The Court Cards," pp. 89–109, for ways to take the Briggs-Myers Type Indicator or alternative ways to ascertain your psychological type.

You may wonder why it is necessary to use a significator at all. Significators are not used just because they have always been used and thus have become traditional or because choosing a card to indicate a specific person makes the reading look more mysterious. The reason a significator is important is because divination works best when your Intuition is allowed to flow with the presence of the moment. Even though synchronicity alone will still draw concordant cards to your own like vibrations, more accuracy and precision may be obtained if you are freed from your normal thought processes and ego-chatter. If, when reading, you can allow yourself to be only in the present, releasing your attachments to the outcome of the situation and to your personal self-image, the archetypal forces can reach through the interdimensional levels to your Intuition with more purity, and thus, more exactitude. And one of the best ways to accomplish this harmonious balance and singularity of purpose is by concentrating on a single significator.

The significator forms a perfect point of focus for the wandering mind and ties it down to an appropriate focal point—not only because an image of yourself naturally sparks your closest feelings—but also because if you are attentive enough and keep forcing your mind to dwell on the visual aspects of the card, this action will help you to clear yourself of other extraneous thoughts and desires. This doesn't, of course, mean that it is sufficient to just look at the significator while thinking of other things. You must actually dwell on it with all your meditative ability.

Using a significator is also helpful because it is a picture of you in the physical, which helps ground less physical forces.

When beginning a reading it is wise to say a mantra or prayer asking for protection and guidance, and to surround yourself with the pure white light of love consciousness. It is important not to have any interruptions, not to be in a hurry, and not to have any sort of time limit set on the reading. If you know you have to be somewhere or do something in a short time, it automatically influences you, causing pressure which disrupts flow. Even if you consciously feel that this doesn't create any pressure, your unconscious knows better, and it is the unconscious you must entertain. For this reason you should wait for a quiet time to do your reading, unobstructed by a time limit or interruptions.

The question to be asked or the issue to be discussed should be chosen carefully. If you ask an ambiguous question you can expect an ambiguous answer. If you ask something like, "Does he like me?", and are unsure of exactly how you mean this, the cards are free to work with the word "like" in any one of several meanings. But if you think very carefully about what you mean, exactly what the issue implies to you, and what you want to know, the cards will respond in like exactness. Of course, there are many times when you may just want to discuss an issue or situation with the cards, being unsure of how you may feel about a certain matter. The cards are excellent for helping you see an issue more clearly. It's like talking the matter over with a wise old friend who simply wants to give helpful advice. In this case, you can let your mind simply flow over the subject while concentrating on the significator. In either case, you should remind yourself that you want the truth of the matter and are willing to accept the answer or advice, regardless of what it may be.

There is no reason to be shy about putting a time reference to the question. If you want to know if something is going to happen within the next week, then ask that. The cards are not anymore vague and general than you are and are quite capable of being as specific and exact as you desire, and surprisingly often, even more so. All things work as reflections of one another, so what you put forth is what you will receive. The reason the cards seem to often give even more than what you ask is because they also use your unconscious.

When you have completely formed the question or subject in your mind, say it out loud in words, verbatim. Stating the question out loud helps to center the energy, clarify the issue, clear up any fuzzy corners, and most importantly, ground the archetype. This can be done while looking at the significator, which is always laid at the center of the reading, and stating the issue in spoken words while shuffling the cards. The significator should be studied in detail, keeping the mind on it, focusing on it, and applying it to the subject that has been asked or stated, all the while shuffling the cards. For as long as the meditation can be comfortably held, keep shuffling the cards and looking at the significator, which is really the physical representation of you or the person being read for. When you want answers brought down to the physical plane, anything physical you can do is helpful, so that the archetypes find it easier to mirror themselves.

During this process sometimes a card will leap out of the deck. If this happens, and it does frequently, lay the card that leaps out face down in the first position, and keep shuffling. If a second card should leap out, put it face down in the second position. If a few cards jump out of the deck put them down in the order of the layout, and then complete the layout when finished shuffling by taking the remaining cards from the top of the deck. It is not unusual to have an entire reading done by cards leaping out of the deck in this way.

The cards should be placed face down and not turned over until all the cards have been shuffled and laid out. The reason for this is that throughout the entire process you should still be meditating on your significator and flowing smoothly with your concentration. If you see the cards that are coming into the reading, you will probably start thinking about them and this causes your mind to begin working again. The mind naturally wants to speculate about the cards it sees, and if it starts wondering or interpreting before the layout is completed, it can impose an attachment to the outcome and break the free-flow of rhythmically forming processes.

There are any number of ways to take the cards from the deck. The most popular way is to take the cards from the top of the deck. Any system will work. The important thing is whichever one you finally end up choosing, stick with it. Be consistent and stay with the same program. With a successful card reading you are working with and laying symmetries to form and harmonize at-one-ment with the archetypes. To present a vague question when a specific answer is desired, or to be unsure of your actions or mode of ritual, brings disrupted patterns with disrupted answers. It is not so much a matter of a correct way to choose or lay out the cards, as it is a matter of maintaining and ensuring the same, consistent methods so that patterns can become established. And since archetypes create themselves out of themselves, the longer you work with the same method, the more re-enforced it becomes with time, continually snowballing to become more and more consistent.

An excellent way to practice and to learn what the cards are saying is to do a daily, weekly, and/or monthly layout. This way you can watch the cards as they play out in your life and come to recognize their meanings. For instance, if you do a weekly reading, you can ask the cards to "show me the following week." A good way to do a weekly reading is to lay the cards out on a Monday morning (Monday being the first day of the week) and do a reading to show the next seven days, including the following Sunday (as Sunday is the seventh day of the week). You don't have to do it on these particular days, but this is the natural flow of weekly time, and, as cannot be overly emphasized, any way you can involve any and all natural patterns will help.

People who have worked with the cards for a while usually find that sometimes they prefer not to know ahead of time "how the cards will fall." They discover that in many instances the future is better left unknown, especially after they've come to develop real confidence in them. After some readers have become good enough to rely on predictions through the cards, they often find they would just rather not know certain things ahead of time. But this precaution comes with time, experience, and knowledge, and in the beginning most people usually want to ask just about everything they can think of, and this is good because it's just about the only way they are really going to learn.

It takes time and practice for most people to really place their trust in divination, and that's the way it should be. The cards are not a weak and obscure system. Faith is not expected without its necessary foundation of knowledge first. In interpretations there is no need to placate anyone with vissitudes, for the cards are strong and have no problem with producing proof if our intentions are sincere. The cards invite being tested and worked with and appreciate our desire for the knowledge they can help bring to us. The archetypes want the individual to gain, for we are all so intricately interwoven that our gain is their gain, and our loss is their loss.

In our culture, many of us have grown up believing that it is wrong to ask God for proof because we should believe on faith. Certainly, faith is paramount, but faith never has, and never will, come from credulity or ignorance. When we fail to *ask* our High Self what we need or want to know, no matter how small or insignificant it may seem to us, we are robbing ourselves of our own very personal and potent connection to God. Every great master and teacher has said over and over again, "Ask, ask, ask, and ye shall receive." It is difficult to believe that God would have us willingly remain ignorant of Its infinite involvement in every aspect of our lives.

The three layouts in this chapter are based on ancient mandalas combined with mystical numerical systems. Each contains a point within the four points of a square, indicating the natural flow of energy in time-space as motion splays down into the physical world, latticing into a Möbius strip to form the four steps of its physical gridwork. This Möbius strip (or figure 8) is seen in mysticism and the tarot, and in traditional decks it is first seen on the 2 of Discs, in Arcanum I either over The Magician's hat or as the form of his hat, and sometimes in Arcanum XI of Strength. At first it is difficult to visualize it in these layouts because the figure 8 represents a holographic energy pattern not technically corresponding with linear structure. However, after you have worked with these layouts for a while you will see that although the spread may be linear, the process the layout foretells will be interdimensional as it plays out in time-space. Each of the three layouts that follow excels in its own way for its own purpose.

THE CROSS LAYOUT

Lay the cards out in the order indicated by the card numbers in figure 1: The Cross (on page 186).

Card #1: The superconscious.
This is the energy coming in from the archetype, or higher code-principle. This is pure energy as yet uncontaminated by physical diffusion. Pauli referred to it as the "indestructible energy." In a reading, this is the energy that is going to be played out through the rest of the cross. Look to it for the theme of the entire reading because it is the energy that the rest of the layout is describing.
(I use the Major Arcana for this card, and the Minor for the rest of the layout, but you don't have to.)

Card #2: The conscious.
This is the energy that is recognized. It is what you are consciously aware of and will personally experience yourself. It will be what you feel, know, do, and what you are in touch with. In a reading, this is what you are conscious of.

Card #3: The subconscious.
This is the energy that you are usually unaware of. Because it is the subconscious it may be played out by someone or something else in your environment, as your shadow. It is the synchronicity because what you see on the outer will appear to compliment or oppose what you are on the inner. In a reading, this is what you are usually unconscious of. You may remain unconscious of

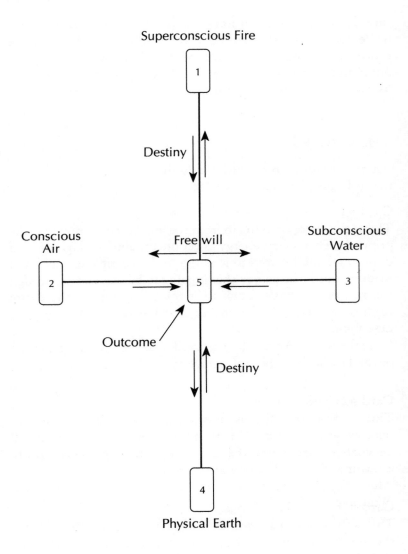

Figure 1. The Cross. The numbers on the cards indicate the order in which they should be laid out, with the 5th card being the pivot point in the center of The Cross.

it, or it may come to play out as an outward event by yourself or another person.

Card #4: The physical.
This is the energy as it manifests on the Earth plane. Oswald Wirth called it the "solution" because it visibly occurs on the Earth plane as the solution to the first three energies on the cross. In a reading, this is what will physically happen in time and space.

Card #5: The outcome.
This is the synthesis of the entire Cross. After all has been said and done this will be the final result. In a reading the synthesis is sometimes recognized immediately. However, it is not unusual for it to take a while to understand the meaning of all that has taken place—hindsight and all that.

It is no accident that the sign of the cross has always been a universal symbol of wholeness and holiness in all cultures throughout history. The cross forms the four steps of energy in the physical world, the natural playing out of energy in all things. The symbol of the cross not only has been and continues to be the sign of wholeness for many religions, but also for countries, organizations, governments, and, of course, mystics.

Oswald Wirth refers to a form of a cross layout in his book *The Tarot of the Magicians*[2] and mentions its magical function. The most popular and traditional layout known to all carto-mancers everywhere is The Celtic Cross, which is based on the cross. In his book *Synchronicity: The Bridge Between Matter and Mind*, F. David Peat discusses in length Carl Jung's and Wolfgang Pauli's experiences with the expression of energy as symbolized in the cross. In their experiences with the cross and Pauli's World Clock, they describe the universal subconscious

---

[2]Oswald Wirth, *Tarot of the Magicians* (York Beach, ME: Samuel Weiser, 1985), pp. 185–186.

activity of this energy pattern.[3] In most of our activities and beliefs throughout history and on into modern times the cross has remained a veritable cross-cultural holy symbol because it is the four universal steps of energy in all things.

The symbol of the cross as displayed in this Cross Layout allows the cards to express themselves in the most natural of all psychic and physical energy forms. Because of this it is also one of the easiest spreads to read. In this layout the cross is seen in both its parts and as a whole, and this is what makes it so special. Its parts are easily seen, and yet in the end it comes together as one perfect whole. One point of energy cannot be had without its other three counterparts.

The vertical pole of the Cross Layout is called Destiny. The archetypal pure energy is indestructable and unalterable and enters this dimension at the top, then shooting down the vertical pole and splaying out in three directions, across both arms of the Cross and down to the base. In actual reality the energy is not contained in linear direction, but can best be described as following a multi-dimensional figure 8 pattern as it unites in certain completion of its destined symmetry. Energy is in actuality in all space and all movement at the same time, but in the physical plane it can be recognized in its parts by time and visible dimension. The vertical pole of the Cross Layout is called Destiny because the movement of the energy flows from the highest pure archetypal power to ground itself in its inevitable manifestation in time and space. It has been set in motion and *must* complete itself.

The horizontal pole of the Cross Layout is called free will. If people remain unaware and unconscious of the right pole of themselves, they will undergo this part of the Cross as affect and reaction, simply reacting to its action without understanding their own active participation in the events and people in life

---

[3]David F. Peat, *Synchronicity: The Bridge Between Matter and Mind* (New York: Bantam Books, 1987), pp. 10–26.

and what they are doing to cause the course life is taking. They will see the right side of the horizontal pole as people, events, and things that happen to them, believing they have nothing to do with what is happening. But if people take the energy from the left end of the Cross—the conscious—and can bring it across to the right side of the Cross—the subconscious—they cannot change their destiny, but they can alter it.

This change is God's great gift to us. If we will but acknowledge that right side of the Cross as ourselves, and not deny its validity within by projecting it outside of ourselves, we will have the power to alter the energy as it spirals its way down to eventually ground in the physical bottom of the Cross. By virtue of archetypes always being attracted to harmonically-resonant vibrations that oscillate with their own likenesses, if we alter ourselves we will automatically alter our personal environment accordingly.

It is by this vertical right side of the Cross that we can recognize how we are progressing, for if we can see the card there as our self, and not as someone or something else outside ourself, we are becoming more whole. No matter how much we may proclaim we have transformed ourselves and gotten our acts together, if the environment and others in our lives are still in shambles, then we are, too.

THE WHEEL LAYOUT

The Wheel Layout is also called an astrological layout because it looks like the twelve houses in a horoscope. It, too, has as its initial foundation, the cross. When laying out the cards, lay them in the order given in figure 2 on page 190, so that the five cards forming the cross are laid out first (Note the 5th card in the center). Then follow by laying out the rest of the Wheel in the order shown. Although most astrological layouts are done starting with the first house and going around the wheel in

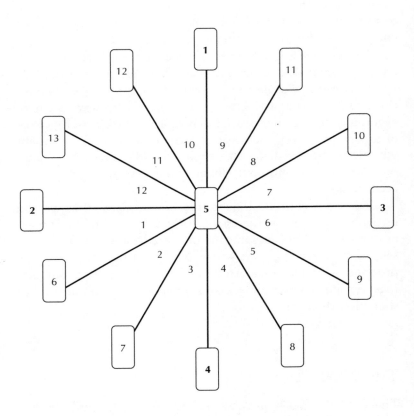

Figure 2. The Wheel. Also called an astrological layout, this reading contains the twelve houses of the horoscope indicated by the numbers in the center of the layout. The numbers on the cards show the order in which they should be laid out, beginning with the five cards that make up The Cross (in bold).

order, this one is not, because we want to maintain the four points of the cross (and their meanings) by laying the cross out first. In this way we retain the meaning of the cross as well as using the traditional astrological meanings of all twelve houses.

In astrology there are twelve houses. The Wheel is based on these twelve houses, and the astrological meanings apply to reading the cards. [The numbers of the houses are indicated on the inside of the Wheel.] Each house applies to a certain area of life. For instance, if you get the 10 of Discs in the 8th house, you might expect to be receiving money from other people because the 10 of Discs is sometimes money, and the 8th house rules other people's money. If you get the 9 of Swords in the 6th house, you might possibly become ill, because the 9 of Swords can indicate sickness, and the 6th house rules health. On the other hand, if you get the 9 of Wands in the 6th house, you can look forward to good health. The following list gives an overview of what the twelve houses mean in astrology:

1st House: yourself; your health; your car; ego; personality; your physical body in general; how you see things; your conscious mind; head and eyes in particular.

2nd House: your earned income—money you earn yourself; Your values; money; food; resources; ears, hearing, neck, throat, lower jaw.

3rd House: communication; siblings; writing and speaking; teaching and learning; your car again; logic and thinking; school (through high school); short trips; hands, arms, shoulders, lungs.

4th House: your home; your mother; foundation; base; your family; real estate; how things end; stomach, breasts.

5th House: all children in general; first child; love in all forms— love affairs, love of children, love of creativity or expression of love; love of spirituality; hobbies; self-expression; upper back and heart.

6th House: work; labor; service to others; food; duties and responsibilities; your pet and small animals; your health again; co-workers; your job; intestines.

7th House: your mate; your Shadow; your unconscious mind; business partner or partners of all kinds; lower back and kidneys.

8th House: death; other people's money; taxes and insurance; sex; transformation; control; the occult; genitals, excretory system, and reproductive system.

9th House: spiritual seeking, inspiration; the house of God; wisdom; religion; long trips and foreign travel; higher education (beyond public school); hips, thighs and buttocks.

10th House: your career; your father; authority figures; the establishment; policemen; the boney system, especially knees; the skin, hair, teeth.

11th House: hopes, goals and wishes; groups, clubs and organizations; friends; legs from below knees through ankles.

12th House: the unconscious; lives before this one, the last life in particular; karma; what we don't know; hospitals and institutions; feet; lymph system.[4]

This spread is also good for doing yearly forecasts. A great way to start the New Year is to do the Wheel for the year ahead. When doing a yearly forecast the first card in the 1st house represents January, the second card in the 2nd house represents February, and on around the Wheel, until you get to the twelfth

[4]Some of these descriptions are taken from Edwin C. Steinbrecher, *The Inner Guide Meditation* (York Beach, ME: Samuel Weiser, and London: Aquarian Press, 6th edition, 1988), p. 250.

card in the 12th house for December. You can start with any month, making the 1st house and the first card the month you are currently in. It is more harmonically sound, however, to start with January as the first month. When doing the Wheel for a yearly forecast do not lay the cross out first because in this case you're wanting to know a specific time factor for each month of the year. Start with house #1 and go around the Wheel in order, making the first card laid out in the 1st house and on around until the twelfth card is laid out in the 12th house. The thirteenth card laid upon the significator in the center gives you the general theme for your entire year.

THE GYPSY SPREAD

This is a layout based on Marthy Jones' Basic 52 Card Reading in her book *It's in the Cards*. She says that this spread is popular among gypsies because it is easy to remember. It is a fifteen card layout, and may appear extremely simple, but there are 7,921,834,931,684,532,412,560,000 possible variations![5] The layout shown here is basically the same but I interpret the cards somewhat differently. See fig. 3, page 194.

Center: Card #1 in the center represents the person being read for, so the reader places the significator here before laying out the rest of the cards. Cards 2 and 3 also represent the person being read for and are the first two cards laid out after shuffling. These are the key cards in the situation and provide extended information about yourself, how you feel about the question, how you are interacting with the situation, and the general nature of the entire reading.

---

[5]Marthy Jones, *It's In the Cards* (York Beach, ME: Samuel Weiser, 1984), p. 7.

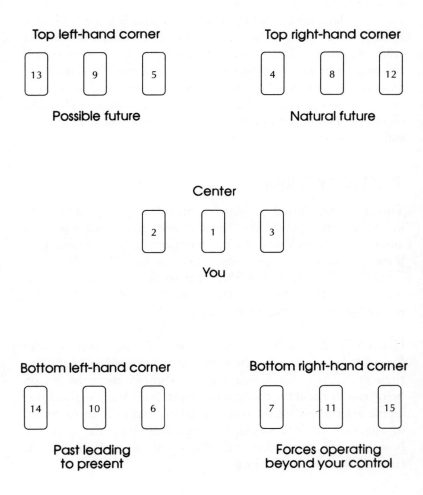

Figure 3. The Gypsy Spread. This fifteen-card spread is easy to remember yet just as accurate as other readings. The numbers indicate the order in which the cards should be laid out, beginning with the center.

Top Right-Hand Corner: The natural future. These cards show the direction that the situation will naturally follow unless some action is taken to change its course.

Top Left-Hand Corner: The possible future. These are the possibilities for alternative action, which may be desirable or undesirable, depending on the other cards in the layout and what you want. Sometimes the future will involve both these cards *and* the cards in the top right-hand corner, depending upon the reading.

Bottom Left-Hand Corner: Elements from the past which influence the future. This is the section that describes the circumstances or ideas from the past that have formed the basis for your present situation.

Bottom Right-Hand Corner: These show forces operating beyond your control, which cannot be changed, but to which you can adapt. They include circumstances, influences, people, and external forces outside your control. If positive, no problem; if negative, they can be put to good use when handled properly.

This is a great layout to demonstrate the free will or lack of free will we may or may not have in our life. The possible future in the upper left-hand corner in conjunction with the natural future in the upper right-hand corner enables you to see alternatives in your life. This layout really has to be done and experienced to see how clearly this is exhibited, and how you either do or do not have the choice to choose how you handle a situation that comes up in your possible future. It is endlessly fascinating to watch how you and everyone you know plays out and responds to the two different futures that the cards present.

Final Thoughts on Tarot Divination

Different people explore the tarot for different reasons. Just like any other field of endeavor, it contains as many different kinds of goals as there are people. There are curiosity seekers, escapists, power seekers, students, God seekers, the humble and the troubled, and the knowledge lovers. Some of us study the tarot because we are dissatisfied with our lives and something nags at us that things exist beyond what we are told and what we have seen, and the way out of our lackluster lives seems to be to seek God, or powers beyond our own. If society, science, and our conscious selves have failed to provide us with peace, then sometimes our own unconscious leads us back to a road that takes us further within, where perhaps we may discover how to love better and to be loved, how to accomplish what it is we have secretly dreamed of, or how to heal the aching emptiness that other methods have failed to remedy.

In the beginning, we may approach tarot as just another crutch, something else to lean on to cure what we have not been able to cure for ourselves. We look to it as we have to other previous paths we have undertaken, hoping that this time the great powers of the vast unknown will carry us—take responsibility for us. But we soon discover that all paths lead nowhere, and tarot is just like all other paths—if we stick with tarot long enough and pursue it sincerely, it will eventually lead us back face to face with ourselves.

It has been said that the goal is not at the end of the path, but the path itself, and tarot offers so many unexpected rewards and surprising gifts along the way that almost immediately after embarking upon tarot, we realize how true this is. Many of these experiences are too individualistic or non-translatable to render in words and can only be hinted at.

When we reach that certain point in our lives and our inner nature begins to interest us, it is not unusual for us to be drawn to some form of divination, and, as we have discussed in this book, tarot can be used to better understand ourselves and others. Tarot offers the persistent seeker previously undreamed of realities and opens up worlds (both inside and outside) that might not otherwise be discovered.

One boon of divination, *if done correctly*—as opposed to some other more socially acceptable paths—is that divination shows us that, although it is not going to make us into what we are not and it is not going to solve our problems, it can prove to us beyond any shadow of a doubt that there is order in the Universe. It does this in innumerable ways—inevitably, unfailingly—and this experience must be lived, for it cannot be explained. After we work with the cards for a while, if we are doing it right, we see that they are correct, all-seeing, more knowledgeable of our past, present, and future than even we are. And if something as simple, uncomplicated, and unscientific as laying out a deck of cards after merely shuffling them can contain such precision and order, then we may surmise that there is something big behind it.

Divination can show us order in the Universe and in our own lives and can prove that this order is perfect, that it never falters, that it is omniscient in its plan. Through the constant use of divination, we eventually come to accept that nothing happens by chance or accident.

For most of us, a belief in a perfect order is synonymous with believing in God, or The All, or Spirit, or whatever we label those benevolent higher forces which exist beyond our five senses and our human understanding. We may sometimes not like the order, but seeing and proving to ourselves over and over again that the cards, without regard to time, space, or human intervention, are infallibly accurate may convince some of us that there exists a God whose order and plan is exceedingly well devised.

Reading the cards is a process that even the most discriminating and dedicated readers regard with respect and wonder. Many of us unconsciously have the idea that we are using the cards and archetypes as channels. This is only partially the case. It is perhaps more appropriate to say that the archetypes are using us as channels.

In the physical state, where we exist now, we perceive division, separation, and multiplicity of the One. However, in the pure, uncontaminated God state, God and life are One and wholly undivided. Symmetries, the Gods, or the archetypes, are the ways through which energy is released out of the infinite into the finite. Archetypes are a mirror for the Eternal, and through the laying out of cards, we may see a small portion of this mirror as it is being reflected in us. We all reflect each other. As above, so below.

If, as a diviner, you possess the honesty of mind and trust of spirit to surrender to a knowledge and power higher than your own, turning your love of self over to a greater love for God, then the act of divination may lead to that special and rare moment when you are both the perceiver and the perceived.

If, in a creative moment of divination, you—the diviner— can sense the timeless moment in which all distinctions vanish, out of this moment you may perceive the miracle of truth. Above all else, when the self releases its attachment to its own isolated ego, to its own needs, fears, judgments, and opinions, then creative awareness can occur, vision stretches into your field of perception, and you truly divine.

Bibliography

Baer, Randall N. & Vicki V. *The Crystal Connection*. New York: HarperCollins, 1987.

Briggs-Myers, Isabel, with Peter B. Myers. *Gifts Differing*. Palo Alto, CA: Consulting Psychologists Press, 1980.

Butler, Bill. *Dictionary of the Tarot*. New York: Schocken Books, 1975.

Carey, Ken. *Notes to My Children: A Symplified Metaphysics*. Kansas City, MO: Uni-Sun, 1984.

Cirlot, J.E. *A Dictionary of Symbols*. New York: Philosophical Library, 1971.

Crowley, Aleister. *The Book of Thoth*. York Beach, ME: Samuel Weiser, 1974.

Dummett, Michael. *The Game of Tarot*. London: Gerald Duckworth & Co., Ltd., 1980.

Fairfield, Gail. *Choice Centered Astrology: The Basics*. Seattle, WA: Ramp Creek, 1990.

Goodman, Linda. *Star Signs: The Secret Codes of the Universe*. New York: St. Martin's Press, 1987.

Greer, Mary K. *Tarot For Your Self*. North Hollywood, CA: Newcastle, 1984.

Hall, Manly Palmer. *The Secret Teachings of All Ages*. Los Angeles: The Philosophical Research Society, 1977.

Hoeller, Stephan A. *The Gnostic Jung and the Seven Sermons to the Dead*. Wheaton, IL: Theosophical Publishing House, 1982.

Holy Bible. King James Version. Cleveland: The World Publishing Company.

Jones, Marthy. *It's in the Cards*. York Beach, ME: Samuel Weiser, 1984.

Jung, C.G. *The Archetypes and the Collective Unconscious*. Bollingen Series XX, translated by R.F.C. Hull. Princeton, NJ: Princeton University Press, 1968.

_____. *Memories, Dreams, Reflections*. New York: Random House, 1965.

_____. *Psychology and the Occult*. Princeton, NJ: Princeton University Press, 1976.

_____. *Psychological Types*. Bollingen Series XX, translated by R.F.C. Hull. Princeton, NJ: Princeton University Press, 1971.

_____. *Synchronicity: An Acausal Connecting Principle*. Bollingen Series XX, translated by R.F.C. Hull. Princeton, NJ: Princeton University Press, 1973.

Kaplan, Stuart R. *The Encyclopedia of Tarot, Volume I*. Stamford, CT: U.S. Games, 1983.

Knight, Gareth. *The Treasure House of Images*. Rochester, VT: Destiny Books, 1986.

Nichols, Sallie. *Jung and Tarot: An Archetypal Journey*. York Beach, ME: Samuel Weiser, 1980.

Noble, Vicki. *Motherpeace: A Way to the Goddess*. San Francisco: HarperCollins, 1983.

Ouspensky, P.D. *Tertium Organum: A Key to the Enigmas of the World*. New York: Vintage Books, 1982.

Parker, Derek & Julie. *The Compleat Astrologer*. New York: McGraw Hill, 1971.

Peach, Emily. *The Tarot Workbook*. London: Aquarian Press, 1984.

Peat, F. David. *Synchronicity: The Bridge Between Matter and Mind*. New York: Bantam Books, 1987.

Regardie, Israel. *The Golden Dawn*. St. Paul, MN: Llewellyn Publications, 1984.

Sadhu, Mouni. *The Tarot*. North Hollywood, CA: Wilshire Book Company, 1968.

Sharman-Burke, Juliet, and Greene, Liz. *The Mythic Tarot.* New York: Simon & Schuster; and London: Random Century (Rider), 1986.

Steinbrecher, Edwin C. *The Inner Guide Meditation.* 6th edition. York Beach, ME: Samuel Weiser; and London: Aquarian Press, 1988.

Swimme, Brian. *The Universe is a Green Dragon.* Santa Fe: NM: Bear & Company, 1984.

Walker, Barbara G. *The Secrets of the Tarot.* San Francisco: Harper Collins, 1984.

Wang, Robert. *An Introduction to the Golden Dawn Tarot.* York Beach, ME: Samuel Weiser, 6th printing, 1987.

———. *The Qabalistic Tarot.* York Beach, ME: Samuel Weiser, 1983.

Wanless, James. *New Age Tarot: Guide to the Thoth Deck.* Carmel, CA: Merril-West Publishing, 1988.

———. *The Voyager Tarot Deck.* Carmel, CA: Merril-West Publishing, 1985.

———. *Voyager Tarot: Way of the Great Oracle.* Carmel, CA: Merril-West Publishing, 1989.

Wirth, Oswald. *The Tarot of the Magicians.* York Beach, ME: Samuel Weiser, 1985.

Jana Riley has been studying esoteric subjects since 1974. She is a graduate of Indiana University, with a B.S. in Business. Since 1976, she has owned and operated a small advertising firm, while teaching astrology classes and workshops, lecturing locally, and working with charts and tarot cards for many clients. Ms. Riley lives in Indiana with her son, Ryan. She is the author of *Tarot Dictionary and Compendium*, also available from Samuel Weiser, Inc.